The Mysteries of the
"Frenchman's Map"
of Williamsburg, Virginia

(Frontispiece). The George Wythe House. Abutting
on the Bruton churchyard and overlooking Palace
green, the Wythe House was Rochambeau's headquarters from November 15, 1781, to July 1, 1782.

The Mysteries of the
"Frenchman's Map"
of Williamsburg, Virginia

By

ALAN SIMPSON

The Colonial Williamsburg Foundation
Williamsburg, Virginia

Library of Congress Cataloging in Publication Data

Simpson, Alan, 1912–
    The mysteries of the "Frenchman's map" of Williams-
burg, Virginia.

    1. Plan de la ville et environs de Williamsburg en
Virginie. I. Colonial Williamsburg Foundation.
II. Title. III. Title: "Frenchman's map" of Williams-
burg, Virginia.
GA460.W55S56   1984   912'.7554252   83-26361
ISBN 0-87935-104-7

Printed in the United States of America

Acknowledgments

Many obligations to librarians, scholars, and friends for access to maps, permission to use manuscripts, tips on solving historical puzzles, and general wisdom have been mentioned in the course of this essay.

Thanks are due here to Carlisle H. Humelsine, chairman of the board, and Charles R. Longsworth, president, of the Colonial Williamsburg Foundation for their encouragement of this research; to members of the departments of Archaeology, Archives and Records, Architectural Research, Audiovisual Programs, Collections, and Research for invaluable counsel; to Mrs. Rutherfoord Goodwin for a masterly review of the staff research of the previous generation; to Paul Buchanan for unique insights into the graphics of the map; to the curators of manuscripts at the College of William and Mary for aid in examining the map; to James N. Haskett, senior historian, Colonial National Historical Park, Yorktown; to J. Richardson Dilworth, General Delmas, M. Jacques Bachy, Mlle. Monique Pelletier, Mlle. Nelly Lacroq, and Mme. P. H. Bonnel for introductions to historical collections in Paris; and to three companions in historical detection, Helen Byrd, Joy Rowe, and Mary Simpson.

Contents

Illustrations

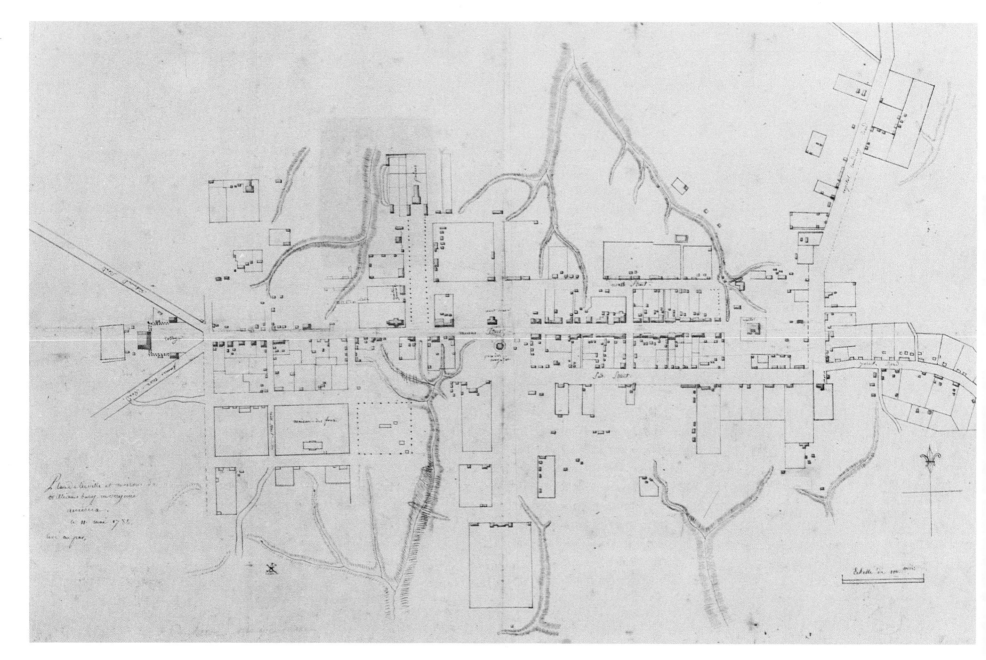

Figure 1. The Frenchman's Map.

Six Unsolved Puzzles

Hundreds of maps must have been drawn by Frenchmen who served in General Rochambeau's American campaigns between June 1780 and December 1782—reconnaissance maps, maps of marches, maps of campsites, billeting maps, town maps, maps of fortifications, sieges, and battles, maps of every description from hurried field sketches to the finished masterpieces intended for the collections of a general or a king. Scores of these maps can be seen today in the libraries of the United States, France, and Britain. But only one of them is known in Williamsburg circles as the "Frenchman's Map."

This is a town plan of Williamsburg showing the entrance roads, the three main streets and the cross streets, the heads of the creeks and ravines, the house lots with fences around them, and most of the buildings inside or outside the fences, each marked by a scaled rectangular block. Several public buildings, such as the College of William and Mary at the west end of the long main street, the Capitol at the east end, the Palace on the north, the Public Hospital in the south, and the Courthouse of 1770 and Powder Magazine in the middle, are indicated by name. Bruton Parish Church and a windmill at the foot of Mill Street are shown by unmistakable diagrams. It is a manuscript map, $25\frac{1}{2} \times 16\frac{1}{2}$ inches, in pen and ink and color with the title, scale, and about half of the place-names in French, the other half in English. It is well drawn but clearly unfinished; an austere, spare-looking map without much ornament but grown quite beautiful through the cosmetics of age, with all its little faded terra-cotta blocks among the spidery creeks. (*Figure 1*)

The owner of the map is the College of William and Mary. A facsimile reproduction, commissioned by the Colonial Williamsburg Foundation in 1941 and printed by the Meriden Gravure Company of Meriden, Connecticut, hangs in many of the public rooms and offices of the Foundation. A later reproduction is for sale at the Information Center.

The Frenchman's Map is not the most brilliant of the maps drawn by Frenchmen in the Revolutionary War. Colonel Jean Desandroüins's great "Map of the Environs of Williamsburg," which is the pride of the collection of Rochambeau maps at the Library of Congress, might claim that honor. Desandroüins was the commanding officer of the royal engineers. Two maps of Rhode Island, one by the veteran Desandroüins, the other by two gifted young men in their twenties from a distinguished mapmaking family, the Berthier brothers, Alexandre and Charles, would also be contenders. There are very spectacular maps of the siege of Yorktown drawn as gallery maps by the French engineers.[1]

The Frenchman's Map, however, has had an extraordinary history. When John D. Rockefeller, Jr., embarked on the restoration of Colonial Williamsburg in 1926, the map was quickly hailed as the "Bible of the Restoration" because of the unique guidance it provided for the long-forgotten foundations of the eighteenth-century town. It has also established itself as a mystery map because of the way in which several basic questions about its identity have eluded solution. It has been like one of those bottles of mystery wine that the host of a dining club produces to challenge the learned palates of his companions, who then sip, ponder, exchange knowing looks, and make their guesses. Here there has been no host or anyone else privy to the secret who could have the last word.

The Frenchman's Map has resisted this sort of wine tasting for seventy years. There have been lots of guesses, and some guesses have been more popular than others, but the experts have never agreed on the answers to as many as six fundamental questions: when the map was drawn, why it was drawn, how it was drawn, how it was actually used, who was its author, and what happened to it after the French left America.

It was a special interest of the author's in the French cartography of the Yorktown campaign, aroused by an unfinished map[2] of the peninsula that the Berthier brothers had drawn in Williamsburg during the winter of 1781–1782, that led to a reexamination of the Frenchman's Map. Various puzzles connected with Washington's routes from Williamsburg to Yorktown had suggested new photography of the Berthier map, and in the midst of this detective work it came as a great surprise to discover that the celebrated Frenchman's Map might rival Winston Churchill's description of "a riddle wrapped in a mystery inside an enigma."

Had the time come to take a new look at these old puzzles? The temptation to plunge in was irresistible.

The Bible of the Restoration

The map had been given to the college in January 1909 by a New York City contractor, John D. Crimmins, who made a hobby of collecting old maps, having found that their information about swamps and streams before everything was paved over on Manhattan was a valuable guide in his business. He was persuaded to return this Virginia map to its rightful home by a relative of the family who lived in Williamsburg, Mrs. Betty Custis Ambler. His brief letter to Mrs. Ambler referred to the date of the map as May 11, 1786, and asked her to give it to the librarian of the college with his compliments.[3]

Almost all that was ever discovered about the previous history of the map was preserved in a recollection of Miss Emily Pryor Christian, a member of the modest library staff in 1909—perhaps its only member—who was consulted in 1935 after the map had become famous. She thought that Mr. Crimmins had "acquired it from someone who had taken it during the War Between the States."[4]

Miss Christian also recalled that Mrs. Ambler had given the map to the president of the college, Dr. Lyon G. Tyler. It might have been expected that some comment of Dr. Tyler's would have been preserved. It was little more than a year since he had published a notable history of *Williamsburg, The Old Colonial Capital*, which included as its frontispiece a map entitled "Map of Williamsburg About 1790, From The Original In The College Library." How could he have repressed his excitement when he compared his town plan of house lots and their owners with the actual buildings as shown on the Frenchmen's Map? But if there is any trace of this in his papers, it has never been found. We are only told that he had the new acquisition neatly framed and hung in the library.

Either Miss Christian or Dr. Tyler must have been the source of the tradition, preserved in the facsimile reproductions, that Mr. Crimmins had bought the map in Norfolk, Virginia. College archives have nothing to say about this. The Crimmins Contracting Company, founded in 1848, is now in its fifth generation in New York City, and the grandson of John D. Crimmins, David Challinor, is assistant secretary for science at the Smithsonian Institution. Responding to an inquiry, he wrote, "I only wish I had more to add. My mother and her younger sister were with my grandfather when he bought the small library in Norfolk. As I remember the story from her, the map was inserted in one of the books and did not actually turn up until the collection he had purchased had reached New York. When he learned what he had, he gave the map to William and Mary to honor his daughter-in-law Margaret Custis Crimmins who was related through the Custises to George Washington."[5]

Eighteen years passed. In November 1926 the Reverend W. A. R. Goodwin, the man with the vision who inspired the man with the money, was told by Mr. Rockefeller to think big. It was Goodwin who had restored Bruton Parish Church when he was rector there in the early years of the century, but he had gone to St. Paul's in Rochester, N. Y., in 1908. When he returned to Williamsburg in 1923, he plunged into more restoration activities with projects like the George Wythe House and the Powder Magazine. But it seems that it was only after Mr. Rockefeller had signaled his conversion to the grand design of restoring the whole city that Dr. Goodwin discovered—or became fully conscious of—the existence of the Frenchman's Map.

He must have spent a frenzied Christmas.

In a letter to Mr. Rockefeller dated January 11, 1927, he described his researches:

Since writing to you last the Colonial Williamsburg Restoration project has been very constantly in my mind, and I have found out quite a number of very interesting things.

After mentioning that his secretary had spent part of her Christmas vacation in the Library of Congress seeing what she could learn from old *Virginia Gazettes*, he continued:

We have found an old map at the College of Williamsburg in 1782. This map locates every house in Williamsburg at that date. It is drawn to scale, and was drawn by a French military officer. It marks the Wythe House as General Headquarters. This map will be invaluable in our study.[6]

Dr. Goodwin outlined several other discoveries and then explained that William G. Perry of the Boston architectural firm of Perry, Shaw and Hepburn would begin talks with him in Williamsburg the next day. At this stage, all was tentative and highly secret. It was not until June 1928 that Dr. Goodwin held a famous mass meeting to announce the name of the donor and the scope of the master plan.

The impatience of the architects to photograph the Frenchman's Map can easily be imagined. But it was like wooing a maiden guarded by a dragon. The librarian of the college, Dr. Earl Gregg Swem, was a learned and lovable bibliophile, but as an Iowan adopted by Virginia he was more protective of southern values than most Virginians. He refused to allow the map to be photographed on the grounds that with only a few exceptions the staff were northern men who had no conception of Virginia history, either past or present.[7] Dr. Goodwin then had the bright idea of asking his assistant, John B. Bentley, a young missionary from Alaska who got on with Dr. Swem and could draw a map, if he could wangle permission to make a copy. They figured that with all his exposure to cold weather in Alaska he would be able to tolerate the drop in temperature that occurred when anyone mentioned the Restoration to Dr. Swem.

"I went to see Dr. Swem," said the young man many years later when he was dictating his reminiscences as the Bishop of Alaska, "and he received me courteously—I can't say warmly—he frowned and scowled and hesitated, but as time went on he relented. Finally he said that I might copy the map if I did it in the library . . . provided I didn't put a pencil or tool of any sort on the map itself and would assure him that it would suffer no harm."[8]

He made his copy. Several hundred blueprints were run off. Dr. Swem was thanked for his cooperation. Colonel Arthur Woods, Mr. Rockefeller's right-hand man in his Williamsburg adventure, said that Mr. Rockefeller would like to show his appreciation. But Mr. Bentley refused to accept anything, saying that it was all done on Bruton Parish's time. "Well," said Colonel Woods, "I'll find some way." On his return to Alaska Mr. Bentley found that $2,000 had been deposited by Colonel Woods to his personal account, which he then transferred to a missionary account so that he could spend it with a good conscience. "When it was gone, I wrote to Colonel Woods to thank him again, telling him how much help it had been, hoping this might spark some more, but it didn't. He simply wrote and said he was glad it had been a real help."[9]

Before long Dr. Swem was taking as much interest in the Frenchman's Map as the architects themselves and was poring over its puzzles with them. He approved the first batch of photographs in 1930–1931 that was mailed out to the two sons of Mr. Crimmins, to all sorts of experts in the great libraries, and to Warrington Dawson, the Foundation's representative at the American Embassy in Paris, in the hope of clarifying the date, purpose, and authorship of the map and its relationship to other contemporary maps of Williamsburg.[10]

In 1937 Dr. Swem decided to have some more photographs made and some repairs done. Not surprisingly, he was unwilling "to send it off to the Library of Congress or to any firm in the North, for the reason that something might possibly have happened to it," but he felt that W. J. Barrow at the Mariners Museum in Newport News could be trusted.[11]

It would be interesting to know just what repairs were made on that occasion. The map had been twice patched while the French were still using it in Williamsburg, and it is clear from the photographs of 1930–1931 that it was badly creased down the fold running along the axis of Duke of Gloucester Street and worn at the central point. Perhaps these folds were smoothed over—they are never so visible again. If a paste-and-tissue repair was made, it is not obvious to the layman. Perhaps it was on this occasion that the map was backed with the protective fabric that was removed at a later date. This is known to have been a modern repair and not an original linen backing of the kind that the French often gave to their maps because a little window was left in the fabric so that the endorsement on the rear, "Plan De Willamsburg," could be read.[12] But as no record of these repairs was kept, we cannot be sure.

The photographs of 1937 raised new puzzles. Some faint but florid scribbles in pencil at the foot of the map which Dr. Swem had noticed in 1930 now turned out to be some kind of graffiti, in French, of roughly the same period as the map itself. These samples were received with the keenest interest by Rutherfoord Goodwin, the rector's son who was carrying on his father's work, and were promptly sped on their way to the experts. Mr. Goodwin was also allowed to bring Mr. Barrow to the college to take more photographs of the map while it was still out of its frame.

Interest in the Bible of the Restoration reached a climax in the early 1940s. The excitements of the prewar decade as building after building was restored or reconstructed can easily be imagined. In 1937 the famous "Bodleian Plate," with its engraved view of the college, the Governor's Palace, and the Capitol as they were about 1737, was given to Mr. Rockefeller by the curators of the Bodleian Library at the University of Oxford as a mark of their regard for his service to historical education. Dr. Swem was spurred by the reverberations of this great gift to recommend that the college should follow Oxford's example. But it was not to be. Instead, a loan of the map was arranged so that visitors to the Foundation's museum in the Courthouse of 1770 could enjoy an exhibition of the two historic treasures that had done so much for the Restoration. It also seemed highly desirable that the best possible facsimile should be made of the map, both as a celebration of the great achievements of the past decade and as a precaution against the possibility of damage or decay. So the Meriden Company was engaged, engraved titles, seals, and a legend were ordered, and a first edition was printed of 250 numbered copies, which was dedicated to the unknown author of the map "in the hope that his identity may be revealed."[13] Wartime problems delayed the distribution of this edition until 1945. A second edition for general sale was soon forthcoming, which the Meriden Company reproduced by photo-offset lithography. Equally elegant in every other particular, it is thought by the connoisseur not to have quite the same authentic hues of the old manuscript as the first edition.

The next great event in the map's history came in 1972 when a new generation of curators at Swem Library became concerned about its conservation. The Lakeside Press of R. R. Donnelley & Sons, Chicago, contracted to remove the fabric and the adhesive from the back of the map, deacidify the manuscript, repair weak areas from the rear with thin tissue, treat the map with thymol, a powerful disinfectant, and then mount it in plexiglass. Before the map was flown out to Chicago, it was taken by Henry Grunder, the college curator, to the Department of Collections at Colonial Williamsburg and photographed once more. When it returned from Chicago it was housed in a special cabinet, made in Williamsburg to Donnelley's specifications, where it can be admired today by visitors to the Manuscript and Rare Book Department of Swem Library.[14]

During this long history the map had certainly lived up to its reputation as a unique guide to the town plan of Williamsburg at the end of the Revolutionary War. Two generations of architectural historians, general historians, and archaeologists on the Foundation's staff had used it as an indispensable tool for excavation, restoration, and interpretation. John W. Reps, the leading authority on city planning in colonial Virginia and Maryland, helped by the same staff, had also studied it with the greatest care. But much of this work had left the basic questions, which the pioneers had raised with such excitement in the thirties, either unasked or, if asked, unanswered. Nor had any summary of the attempts to answer them ever been compiled.

The first step was to review the folders on the Frenchman's Map in the Foundation's archives and to investigate the college's archives. The next step was to consult the professionals who had worked with the map. As the puzzles identified themselves, recent scholarship in the French military cartography of Rochambeau's American campaigns was examined, and visits were made to most of the libraries in the United States, France, and Britain that owned original manuscripts or good photocopies of these maps and other pertinent records.[15]

As ultraviolet photography had been especially helpful in enhancing the almost invisible details on the original manuscript in Paris of Berthier's unfinished map of the peninsula, Arthur L. Smith, director of the Audiovisual Department, made arrangements through the courtesy of the NASA Langley Research Center for new photography. Elizabeth McCarthy of Boston, Massachusetts, a distinguished handwriting expert, was also consulted. Finally, the manuscript was encouraged to tell its own story in a personal interview, with the help of the interpreter who knows it best, Paul Buchanan, a former director of Architectural Research at Colonial Williamsburg.

Puzzle 1. When Was It Done?

The donor, Mr. Crimmins, believed that the date which appears beneath the title in the bottom left-hand corner of the map was May 11, 1786. The Library of Congress, which has copies of all the major reproductions since 1930, has this date recorded as either 1786, 1782, or 1781. The legend at the foot of the two facsimile editions says, "It is believed that the map was prepared for military purposes in 1781 or 1782, probably the latter, during which period French troops were in action in the vicinity of Williamsburg and, for some time, were quartered there. The inscribed date is, owing to the illegibility of the last digit, open to conjecture."

If each date has had its champions, 1781 and 1786 have been somewhat harder to defend than 1782 because May 11, 1781, was nearly four months before the French forces began to arrive in Williamsburg, and May 11, 1786, was nearly four years after they had left. But this did not deter Dr. Swem, who was himself the editor in chief of a famous index of Virginia historical records, from shifting his opinion from 1786 to 1781. As long as the ambiguous fourth digit looked so unlike the usual figure "2," uncertainty has persisted up to the present day. (*Figure 2*)

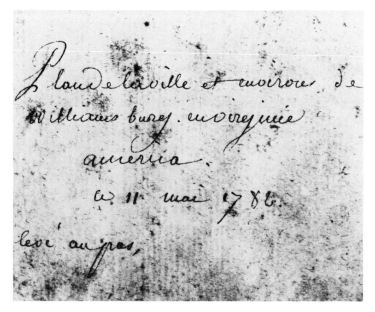

Figure 2. The title of the Frenchman's Map with its puzzling date. Is it 1786, 1782, or 1781?

It was Elizabeth McCarthy who really solved this puzzle by simply asking to see a copybook that was used in eighteenth-century Paris to teach writing. Of course it was the great age of academies and encyclopedias when there was a royal academy to promote the art of writing, and the engraved plates of a grand master like M. Paillasson were used to illustrate the article on calligraphy in Diderot's famous encyclopedia.[16] (*Figures 3a* and *b)* Samples of writing in all its approved forms were quickly forthcoming, but it was a sequence of numerals from 1 to 9, enclosed in a decorative scroll at the foot of an engraved plate by another great master, M. Roland, that cleared up the mystery.[17] After the standard figure "2" of the kind that Desandroüins used when he dated his map of the environs of Williamsburg "1782," or that Dr.

Figure 3a. Capital letters from Paillasson's plates. The "B," "E," and "F" are similar to those used in the graffiti on the Frenchman's Map.

Figure 3b. Conventional numerals, including figures 1, 2, and 6, as illustrated by the writing master, Paillasson. His sixteen plates were published in Diderot's *Encyclopédie.*

Figure 4. Conventional numerals together with variants as illustrated by Roland, another writing master. The variant figure "2" is identical with the ambiguous fourth digit in the date on the Frenchman's Map.

Swem had observed when he looked at Paillasson's plates in Diderot's encyclopedia, M. Roland included a variant "2." *(Figure 4)* The judgment of Elizabeth McCarthy was hardly needed to demonstrate that this is the fourth digit in our cryptic date. Since this discovery several examples of the same usage have been found in a report prepared by a secretary for the signature of a central figure in the mystery story, Brigadier General le Chevalier Pierre François de Béville, Rochambeau's quartermaster general.[18]

So the date on the Frenchman's Map is May 11, 1782. But this can be another red herring if we jump to the conclusion that this was the date of its composition. It could have been put on the map long after its completion. Paul Buchanan astutely pointed out that it could have been done anytime between the arrival of the French troops in Williamsburg in September 1781 and May 11, 1782.

Elizabeth McCarthy then reinforced this line of thought by reporting her findings about the handwriting on the map. She said there were three different hands. One was responsible for almost all the writing on the map itself. A different hand was responsible for the brief description of the map in the bottom left-hand corner, containing the date under discussion, and for the endorsement on the back of the map. And yet a third hand had written the graffiti.

It seemed likely that the titles and the date, and the irreverent doodling, had all been added some considerable time after the map had been drawn and that the date of its composition would only be determined after we had reached some decision about its purpose.

Puzzle 2. Why Was It Done?

Four theories have been advanced over the years.

1. It is a billeting map, connected in some way with the winter quarters occupied by French troops in Williamsburg between about November 15, 1781, and July 1, 1782. This theory has surfaced more often than any other in the guesswork of the years, but it has also sunk from time to time.

2. It was a diversion for some officer who enjoyed drawing maps and had plenty of time in which to indulge his hobby. Baron de Turpin, for example, was one of Desandroüins's royal engineers who took a trip to the mountains in May 1782 and came back with some fine sketches of the famous "Natural Bridge" that were published in 1787 in the Marquis de Chastellux's *Travels in North America*.

3. It was a preliminary draft for one of the great showpiece maps such as those drawn for Rhode

Island in the fall of 1780 by Desandroüins or the Berthier brothers.

4. It was a training exercise to keep the engineers usefully occupied during their idle months in Williamsburg.

Of these theories, the first might seem the most plausible, but no attempt has ever been made to substantiate it or to meet various skeptical doubts that students of the map have raised. If it is a billeting map, why does not the title say so? Why is there no evidence, such as a key, to show which buildings are to be used for billeting? Why are all sorts of little buildings shown which could never have been used for billets? Why is the Public Hospital (*Maison des Foux*) with an obvious utility as a barracks left unfinished?

Above all, how can the theory of a billeting map be reconciled with any one of the three supposed dates on the map? It is totally incompatible with 1786, and only consistent with May 1782 on the assumption, for which there is no evidence whatever, that the settlement of claims for compensation called for such a map at that time. As for May 1781, Dr. Swem's final inclination for reasons of calligraphy, this can only be defended on the assumption that Lafayette, who was tailing Cornwallis, thought that a map of Williamsburg might come in handy sometime and sent someone to draw it. This was over a month before Cornwallis himself reached Williamsburg, and over two months before he had any idea that he would end up in Yorktown.

However, there are answers to all these doubts and difficulties which make it necessary to adopt the billeting theory after all.

A comprehensive argument to this effect might begin with the reflection that Rochambeau was bound to have directed his engineers to draw a map of a town that he was proposing to make the center of his winter quarters and to occupy for six months or more. Williamsburg was not big enough, as Newport had almost been, to absorb his whole army of five thousand. He had to find additional accommodation at Hampton, Yorktown, the Half-Way House between these two towns, Gloucester, Jamestown, and West Point. But the generals and their staffs, the engineers, the supply services, the medical service, and the wounded, the whole of the Bourbonnais Regiment, seven companies of the Royal-Deux Ponts Regiment, and most of the artillery except siege guns at West Point and a few other guns at Yorktown, found places for themselves in Williamsburg.[19] If there must have been a map, surely this map should be regarded as the obvious candidate, once all the obstructions created by confusions about its dating have been removed. With Puzzle 1 solved as indicated, there is no reason why this map should not have been drawn at the time required for a billeting map, namely, as soon as possible after Cornwallis had surrendered.

Next, there is a strong family resemblance between this map and the only two fully authenticated billeting maps that have survived from this campaign, one of which is for Hampton and the other for Yorktown. The original manuscripts of these maps have been among the Berthier papers at Princeton University Library since the 1930s,[20] but they were first reproduced in a wonderful contribution to the general literature of French military cartography that appeared in 1972—two meticulously edited and beautifully illustrated volumes by Howard C. Rice, Jr., and Anne S. K. Brown, *The American Campaigns of Rochambeau's Army, 1780, 1781, 1782, 1783.*

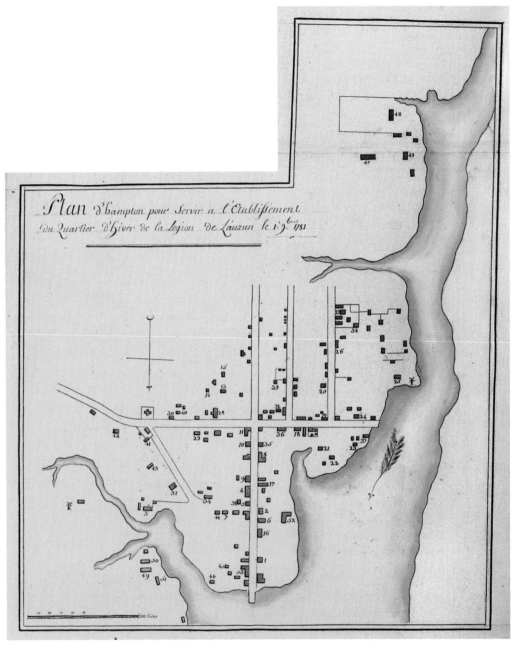

Plan d'hampton pour Servir a l'Etablissement
du Quartier d'hiver de la legion de Lauzun le 1.er 9bre 1781

Figure 5. The billeting map for Hampton, Va., as
completed by the Berthier brothers on November
1, 1781. Courtesy, Princeton University Library.

The first to be drawn was the map of Hampton.
(*Figure 5*) The legion of the Duc de Lauzun, made up
of about three hundred cavalry and three hundred
infantry, marched to the northern outskirts of Hampton on October 30, where they camped for a week
until quarters were found for them. They had been
preceded on October 29 by Rochambeau himself who
had come to inspect the proposed accommodation.
We assume that he was accompanied by the brigadier
general de Choisy, who was commanding the legion
in the duke's absence, by de Béville, and by the
Berthier brothers on the latter's staff. Rochambeau
spent the night at Mr. Sheldon's house outside
Hampton and returned to his field headquarters at
Yorktown the next day. The Berthier brothers drew
their map and dated it November 1. The legion
entered their quarters on November 6.[21]

The Yorktown map (*Figure 6*) may have been less of
a problem, given the familiarity acquired during and
after the siege and the extent of the destruction, but
over a week may have passed before the brothers got
down to it, because it is dated November 12. Troops
were already moving in from the battlefield on that
date, although the official entry into quarters was
scheduled for November 15.

These two maps are both simple maps, much
smaller and less complicated than the map of Williamsburg, and could have been executed very
quickly by surveyors as skillful as the Berthiers.
There are signs of haste on the manuscript of the
Yorktown map that are not visible in the Rice and
Brown reproduction; ravines running from the upper
to the lower town are roughly sketched in pencil as if
for later inking and hatching but never picked up.
The two maps differ in one interesting respect. Fifty-
three of the houses on the Hampton map are num-

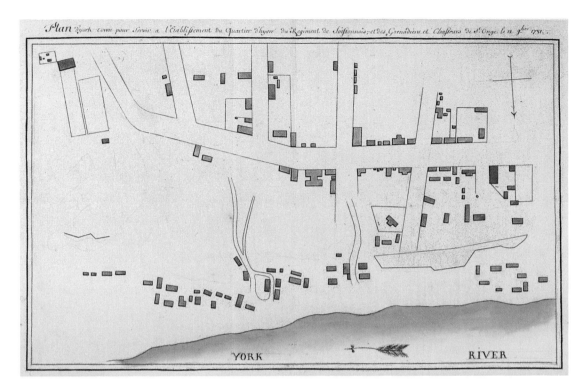

Figure 6. The billeting map for Yorktown, Va. The companion map to *Figure 5* was finished by the Berthier brothers on November 12, 1781. Courtesy, Princeton University Library.

bered, but there are no numbers on the Yorktown map. Otherwise they are unmistakably by the same hand. The formal titles are in the same "display" style. The endorsements on the back of each map, "Hampton" and "York," are in the identical "natural" handwriting. The use of color, which is not reproduced by Rice and Brown, is the same red for the buildings and a bright aquamarine for the river.

There are certain differences between these two maps and the Frenchman's Map, the most obvious being their titles, indicating that each is a plan "to be used for establishing winter quarters" for the named unit or units. Other differences are the absence of place-names and hatching, the use of lines to indicate all streets, and a slightly different symbol for a windmill. But the family resemblance, including a scale of one hundred *toises*,[22] which is roughly three hundred feet to the inch, is so strong as to bring the Williams-

burg town plan clearly within the class of maps that were used for billeting purposes.

Furthermore, if very like the two recognized billeting maps, the Frenchman's Map is in one important respect very unlike almost every other map the French produced in these campaigns. Almost all these surviving maps are "reenactment" maps showing troops on the move, or in fortified positions, or at their stations in the heat of battle. A case in point is the exquisite campsite map of Williamsburg *(Figure 7)* drawn by the Berthier brothers after the event to represent the arrival in Williamsburg of the main column on September 26, 1781.[23] Lafayette's units encamped near the college, and Muhlenberg's units keeping watch over the Yorktown road as it descends to Burwell's mill are clearly marked. There are no military formations on the Frenchman's Map. Desandroüins shows an artillery park near the Powder

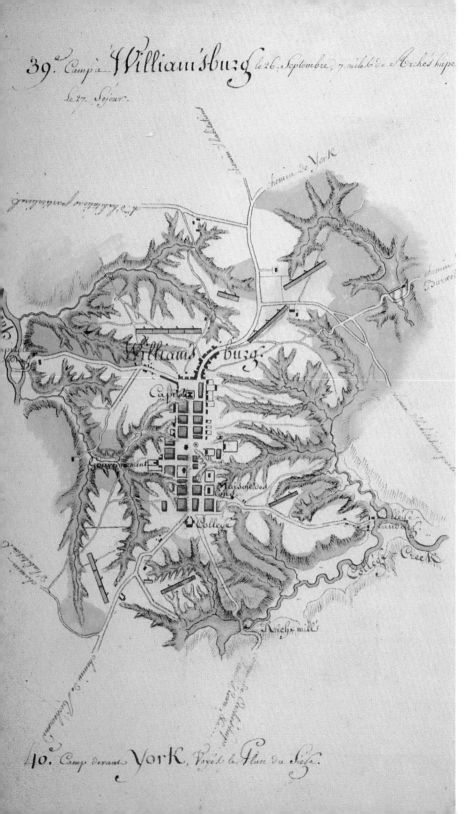

Magazine on his map of Williamsburg. The only symbol on the Frenchman's Map with a military significance is "Quartier General," which is the umbrella description for a headquarter's staff of some sixty officers.

Every other name or symbol on the map denotes a building that was in use as an occupation facility either before or shortly after the early days of November. The President's House at the college was a French hospital, the Palace an American hospital, the Courthouse of 1770 a French barracks, the Powder Magazine an allied facility, Bruton Parish Church a French store, the Public Hospital almost certainly a barracks and store.

Here the argument might rest, with the conclusion that the map's purpose was to help the French with the establishment of their winter quarters, and that its date of composition was sometime after Cornwallis's surrender on October 19 and before the official entry of the troops on November 15, 1781. The question of why it was left unfinished might be resolved, perhaps, with Puzzle 3—"How Was It Done?"

Profanities—Pointless or Otherwise?

A fascinating contingency offers itself at this point. Is it possible, by some wild, improbable chance, that the graffiti at the foot of the map contain a hidden clue to its identity as a billeting map? No one has thought so. Indeed, no one has bothered to translate them precisely since they seemed to be only some soldier's pointless profanities. But what do they mean and how did they get there?

There are two pieces of graffiti. One, at the bottom of the map on the left-hand side below the symbol for

Figure 7. Campsite map of Williamsburg drawn by the Berthiers to represent the arrival of Rochambeau's main column on September 26, 1781. It shows troops of Saint Simon and Lafayette encamped near the college and other units on the east side of the town. Courtesy, Princeton University Library.

the windmill, is just visible on the facsimile editions. The other is at the bottom of the map on the right-hand side, beneath the scale bar, and mercifully invisible.

"Sacré macquereau" *(Figure 8)* might be translated "bloody pimp" or "damned pimp." As such, its only significance for our purposes is the puzzle of its presence.

The second piece *(Figure 9)* is more mysterious. The capital letters are worthy of the most inebriated student in M. Paillasson's classes. The author begins first with a capital "E," then writes the word "Etat" with a bigger capital "E." After that comes a prodigious capital "F" and a word whose ending is missing because the manuscript has been sheared on this side, but the word is undoubtedly "Foutre." Beneath these two words, and almost as floridly inscribed, is "Bougre."

From time immemorial there has been a certain sameness about the military vocabulary. However respectable a man's speech in civil life, the moment he dons the king's uniform he can only express himself in profanities. What the future holds for military speech, now that the worst words have become domesticated and a maiden aunt at her needlework who pricks her finger or drops a stitch can be heard to mutter "foutre," is uncertain. It can only add to the desolation of modern warfare. But in the Revolutionary War, as in World Wars I and II, words like "foutre" and "bougre" were the language of the soldier when he "swore like a trooper," whether he was French or English.

It may be that "foutre," in a heated quarrel, could be peculiarly insulting between men of honor at this time. Alexandre Berthier, the inseparable companion

Figure 8. Graffiti, "Sacré macquereau," scribbled below the symbol for a windmill.

Figure 9. Graffiti, "Etat Foutre Bougre," below the scale bar.

of his younger brother Charles during their American travels and mapmaking, sailed to the West Indies on a different ship when they left Boston in December 1782. Charles got involved in a desperate quarrel with a fellow officer about sharing a sea chest in their cramped quarters and was killed in the resulting duel when they landed at Curaçao. He left a letter for his brother describing the crowning exchange of insults as follows:

When on 4 January he said to me in the rudest tone that it was very strange, but he had been robbed, and that he had had a lock put on the chest and had given a key to no one but me, I did not expect such an outburst and asked him what he meant. He repeated the same thing in a tone that became progressively ruder. It was all I could do to keep from telling him what I thought of him. I asked him if he thought I had robbed him. With much malice, he replied: "Or your servant, at least. I had some apples and a lot of little things I can't find." I almost burst out laughing. I told him that my servant could not have stolen anything, since I had always been present when the chest was opened, and that, besides, he was well known in the regiment, and it was very curious that he should be so rude about this matter. Continuing in the same vein, he ended up by saying, *foutre*, I was an impertinent fool, with such a threatening look that I could not contain myself and retorted with "Well then, *allez vous faire foutre!*" Then, utterly beside himself, he picked up a chair to throw at my head. Fortunately I parried the blow. M. Bazin, who was in his cabin, came in and got between us to prevent me from committing a folly. So that is the provocation that I believe sufficient cause for demanding the life of one of us or the other.[24]

No expert whom I have consulted thinks that "Etat," "Foutre," and "Bougre" in this combination have any coherent meaning. But we are obliged to pause longer over this graffiti than over the other because "état" has a specific meaning that is highly relevant. It means "list" or "inventory" in French military records. "Etat Militaire" is a military list. "Etat des Services" is a service record. And "Etat des Logements" is a billeting list showing where every officer was billeted in a town used for winter quarters.

We shall return to the subject of billeting lists when we reach Puzzle 4—"How Was the Map Used?" Meanwhile, we have to entertain the possibility that before the author of this graffiti subsided into profanity, his eye had fallen on the "Etat des Logements" that normally accompanied a billeting map.

Puzzle 3. How Was It Done?

There is a superficial answer to this question, namely, that it was done without instruments by an anonymous Frenchman who paced the ground ("levé au pas," as the title tells us) and was remarkably accurate in reproducing what he saw in spite of some errors and omissions. Then there is the best possible answer that might be pursued by allowing the map to tell its own story in response to questions that take account of all the observed facts—the paper, the corrections, the variations in scale, the jumble of French and English, the choice of street names, the unfinished portions, the maze of pinpricks, and the graffiti. With luck, each phase of construction might be determined and some defensible conclusion reached as to what sort of draft this was.

A start may be made by suggesting, contrary to the tradition of the single author, that there must have been at least two authors in addition to whatever clerical or other help they might have had.

This assumption is necessary for two distinct reasons, one of which is a curious observation made by Paul Buchanan as far back as the 1950s. He found that the horizontal scale on the Frenchman's Map was consistently longer than the vertical scale. As there is no reason to think that a shrinkage in the paper has produced this effect, the probable explanation is that two men, one with a longer stride than the other, divided their surveying in this fashion. Ezra Stiles, the Congregational minister of Newport, Rhode Island, who later became president of Yale University, drew an excellent street map of Newport by pacing in 1758 and noted at the foot of it, "I suppose about 6 of my paces go to a rod."[25] As the rod is 16½ feet, his pace was 33 inches, which is the pace of a man of medium height. A taller man would have a longer one. So the first thing to be suggested about the authors of the Frenchman's Map is that one was taller than the other!

The next thing is that if one was obviously a Frenchman, the other was almost certainly an American.

The probability that allied teamwork produced the Frenchman's Map has not been considered before, but enough evidence can be assembled to create a very strong presumption.

There is, first, the argument from common sense. Why should French engineers, until very recently complete strangers to the town and now under every kind of pressure to get their winter quarters organized, undertake a survey by themselves? Would they not look to their allies for help?

Secondly, they had used local surveyors in this area before. One of the most fascinating of all the French maps of the Yorktown campaign is a reconnaisance sketch of the routes to Yorktown and the terrain of the coming siege, with a jumble of French notes and English place-names, on which a Frenchman involved in the first rough draft has scribbled "Plan donné par des arpenteurs du pays"—map given by local surveyors.[26]

Thirdly, there is new evidence of the mechanics of allied cooperation in the organization of winter quarters that highlights an official who would have been a very logical source of advice when a Williamsburg surveyor was wanted.

This discovery was first suggested by the Newport precedents of the previous winter, which turned out to be such a treasure-house of clues in our efforts to solve the puzzles of the Frenchman's Map. The discovery that the French used a billeting list, called an "état des logements," which might have stimulated some of the graffiti on the map had come from this source. It now revealed the presence of a billeting officer in Newport called a barrackmaster general whose appointment had been urged by Rochambeau and de Béville and eventually arranged by Timothy Pickering, the American quartermaster general, with Washington's approval.[27] This find prompted a search in Williamsburg for any evidence of a similar appointment in the second winter which was rewarded by the discovery of a remarkable letter, reading in part as follows:

Military considerations have led me, in agreement and with the approval of General Washington and Governor Nelson, to establish the quarters we now occupy. I have waited patiently from the surrender of Lord Cornwallis until now for the winter quarters to be arranged by the town officials of Williamsburg; but the absence of most of them during these troubles, the onset of bad weather, the need for provisions, and the amount of sickness has induced me to appoint a barrack-master general, breveted by General Washington and specially authorized by Governor Nelson, to organize quarters for the sick and for the troops in the least troublesome way for the inhabitants, and to repair at the King's expense all the houses that can be quickly restored for billeting purposes. This is what has happened, and I am very satisfied to see that the grievances complained of have boiled down to the demolition of two run-down huts that had to be destroyed to provide materials for repairs. The individual who owns them has spoken to me and has declared himself very satisfied with the promise I have given him that his materials will be valued and paid for.[28]

Of course Rochambeau himself is the author of this statement. He is acknowledging a lost address of the mayor and councillors, who had waited on him after his arrival at the Wythe House not only to congratulate him on the French contribution to the great victory but also to express their concerns in true English fashion about the billeting of soldiers on private households without the consent of civil authorities. His statement is taken from a copy that he sent to Governor Nelson on November 21 with his assurances that he had managed to satisfy the council. This is the sole surviving reference to the French reliance in Williamsburg on a barrackmaster general comparable to Colonel Jabez Champlin, the ex-sheriff of Newport, who had served them so well in their first winter. The identity of this individual is still unknown, although it might be revealed by a thorough search of Timothy Pickering's papers and those of William Finnie, his deputy quartermaster general in Virginia. But the barrackmaster's availability as someone who could recommend a local surveyor, at a time when Williamsburg was still a largely deserted city, must be acknowledged.

This pyramid of conjecture which points to a joint authorship of the Frenchman's Map may not convince everyone, but it seems plausible enough to be used as a tentative hypothesis. Internal evidence on the map itself, in its mixture of French and English spelling and two misspelled street names that are neither French nor English, offers further support of the same suggestive sort.

We can now try to see how the allied team we are postulating came to produce a map like the Frenchman's Map.

If this map is examined from the rear with a lamp placed in front of it, all sorts of tiny, twinkling stars appear as the light filters through scores of little holes. These are the pinpricks. If they were noticed in the 1930s, no record has survived, but they have been objects of curiosity for many years now. How did they get there? How were they used?

We assume that the two surveyors did their pacing, returned to their plane table with their notes and sketches, reduced them to their scale, and then assembled a first draft of the map on a manuscript the size of the Frenchman's Map, which a clerk had produced by pasting four sheets together.[29] This first draft was presumably in pencil with some names scribbled in. Then, for better accuracy, they made the copy, or second, draft, which is what has come down to us, by pricking the first draft onto a fresh manuscript of the same size, making holes in the corners of the little buildings and along the lines of fences, roads, and trees.

These holes were then connected by pencil to reproduce the original pattern. As traces of ink and red can be seen in some of these holes, they were made before either ink or color had been applied. Further work was then done in pencil, such as the north point, the scale bar, the windmill, and the rough outline of creeks. But less than half the names were scribbled in pencil, and we may guess that these were the work of a Frenchman—"quartier general," "palais," "maison des foux," "College," "Rue du Nord," "means Street," and "Sud Street." (*Figure 10*) There is no indication that the following names were first written in pencil, perhaps because the English surveyor had already scribbled them on the first draft, from which they could be easily copied—"Richmond Road," "Jamestown Road," "mill street," "york Road," "capitol landing Road," "court house," "powder magazine," and "capitol."

Pencil lines and names were then inked in, creeks and hatching added in ink, and all the English names inserted for which there was no previous pencil. But the French surveyor, or clerk, who was doing this had obvious difficulties with the three streets that we think of today as the principal ones—Duke of Gloucester, Nicholson, and Francis. Duke of Gloucester Street was also called Main Street in the eighteenth century, and this was what he was trying to write. If he had been writing it in French he would have written "grande rue," but he tried English and made it "means." He probably did not know, and certainly did not bother, about the names Nicholson and Francis; it was enough that one was north and the other south, so although there is no evidence that

Americans ever called them by these names, that is what they became here.[30] However, North Street was "Rue du Nord" in pencil before he anglicized it in ink as "north Street," and South Street was, and remained, "Sud Street" (*Figure 10*)

This done, the buildings were then colored red with the exception of three areas that were left uncolored: one, the group containing the *Maison des Foux* and the adjacent Custis House; another, the group to the west of the Palace green; and the third, a group along one side of the York road. Why stop before coloring a facility as important to billeting as the *Maison des Foux*? We can only suggest that at this point any hope of making this second draft the final draft was given up. Several errors had already crept in. Two of these had actually been removed by surgery and carefully replaced with patches. Other features, including "Sud Street," had a clumsy look. A ravine too many at the head of one of the creeks had been crossed out. A fence line had been carried into the middle of Francis Street. There were also mistakes in the unfinished areas.

So a third manuscript was prepared and pricking began all over again, though now it was not because the second draft was being constructed from the first but because it was being copied on to the third. In some cases we can see that the original hole was enlarged, but more often a second hole was made near the first. Basically, this is a "double-hole" map, made with one set of holes and copied with another. Buildings in the unfinished areas west of Palace green and along York road were not pricked because there was uncertainty about their accuracy.[31]

If sound, this guesswork establishes the identity of the Frenchman's Map as the second draft of a billeting map, explains how it could have been disfigured

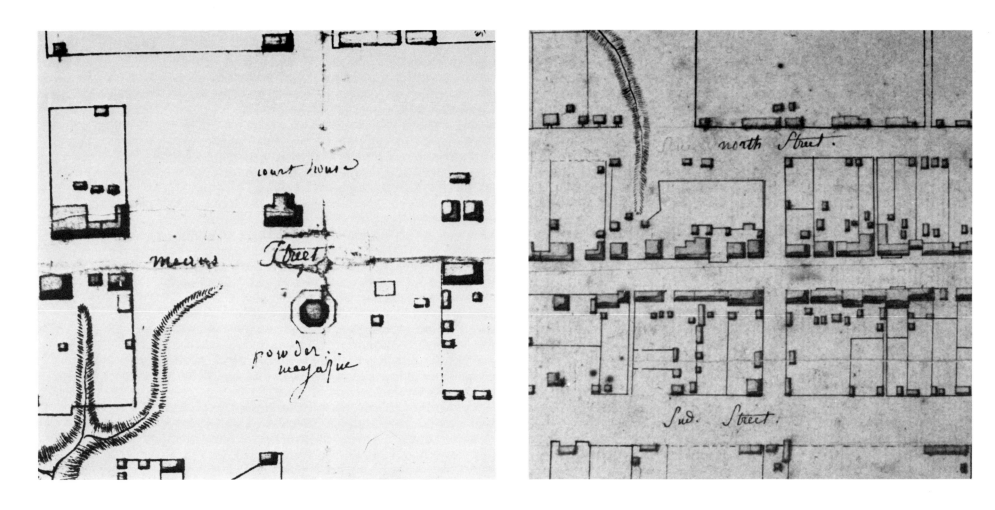

Figure 10. Problem place-names. "Means Street" was meant to be Main Street, an eighteenth-century variant for Duke of Gloucester Street. "North Street" and "Sud Street" were used for Nicholson and Francis Streets. The penciled "rue de nord" can be detected beneath the inked "north street."

with graffiti after it had outlived its usefulness, and leaves no doubt that a more perfect copy was begun, even though no trace of it has survived. We may surmise that a final copy would have carried a title identical in form with the "display" titles of the billeting maps of Hampton and Yorktown.

Puzzle 4. How Was It Used?

This is the place to remove a misconception. The term "billeting map" was invented by Americans, not by the French. The only two fully authenticated maps from Rochambeau's campaigns in America that we have been calling billeting maps were described by their titles as "Plans" of Hampton and Yorktown "to be used for establishing winter quarters." In other words, a billeting map was not a map of billets, but a map of a town in which soldiers were to be billeted. If it were a map of encampments in the field it would show where a particular unit or a headquarters was encamped, but if it were a map of a town selected for winter quarters, although it would show facilities that might be used for a barracks or a hospital or a headquarters, it would not necessarily show where the officers were to be housed. The Yorktown map provided no such information. The Hampton map assigned numbers to fifty-three of the houses, but in the absence of any indication on the map itself, or of any list that might have originally accompanied it, we do not know whether these numbered houses were earmarked for billets or whether they simply represented all the habitable houses in Hampton. It is also conceivable that where an excellent street map of a town was already in the possession of the French, it may have been all they needed to establish their winter quarters, in which case we might speak of that map as their billeting map.

How wonderful it would be if a book of their billeting maps in America, each accompanied by its billeting list, had come down to us from the records of the French quartermaster general! Unfortunately, very few of de Béville's papers for these campaigns have survived. But just as we have two authentic *maps* for the winter quarters in Virginia, so we also have two authentic *lists* for the Rhode Island quarters of the previous winter. And beautifully revealing they are.

The Newport list (*Figure 11*) in its original manuscript occupied a large sheet of paper, about 21 by 16 inches, with ruled columns, entitled "List of quarters (*Etat des logemens*) occupied within the town of Newport by the army under the command of the Comte de Rochambeau during the winter quarters of 1780–1781." The columns were headed "Gentlemen" (*Messieurs*), "Streets" (*Rues*), "Numbers" (*Numéros*) and "At The House Of" (*Chez*). There were three parts to the list. The "Quartier Général" came first, which in this context is best translated "Headquarters Staff." The names and addresses of Rochambeau and the other general officers were at the top, followed by those of the various staffs, such as the aides of each general officer, the royal engineers, the chief artillery officers, and the heads of the various services. It is among just such staff officers that the author of the Frenchman's Map might eventually be identified. Then came "Regiments quartered in the town," in which the names and addresses of the three or four field officers were supplied for each regiment. After that there was a short naval list of senior officers and shore-based facilities with their addresses. The Provi-

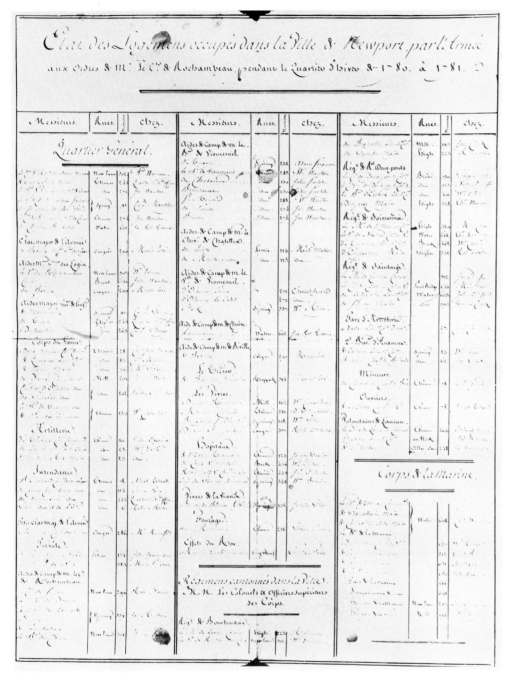

dence list was similar in form, but shorter because it only included the "Quartier Général" and lacked a column for house numbers. It had been prepared for a short stay of about two weeks in June 1781.[32]

If Dr. Swem had ever found such billeting lists for Williamsburg, what might not Colonel Woods have arranged for him? With the solitary exception of the Wythe House, not a single house or tavern in Williamsburg has been definitely identified as the winter residence of a specific French officer. But the Newport list shows where ninety-one officers were quartered.

It was the extraordinary spell of this list that prompted yet another examination of the manuscript sources in Rhode Island to see what more could be learned about the billeting practices of the first winter. The details of these findings have now been published elsewhere,[33] but the essential discoveries are as follows:

The responsibility for finding houses for the French officers was accepted by the town council at an emergency meeting on June 11, 1780—the day that Rochambeau stepped ashore. The local quartermaster on the American side was to be helped by a committee of townsmen to prepare a list. A bargain was struck by Rochambeau whereby the French rank-and-file would be billeted in war-damaged houses, repaired at the French expense, if the townspeople would accept the officers as lodgers in their homes. Colonel Jabez Champlin, acting as a barrackmaster general, numbered over six hundred houses in Newport, supervised the necessary repairs, compiled the Newport billeting list that has survived and other lists for junior officers and men that have not, and sent billeting notices (*Figure 12*) to householders telling them who would be their lodgers.

Figure 11. "Etat des logemens." Billeting list showing the addresses of ninety-one French officers quartered in Newport, R.I., during the winter of 1780-1781. Ryder Manuscripts, John Hay Library. Courtesy, Brown University.

20

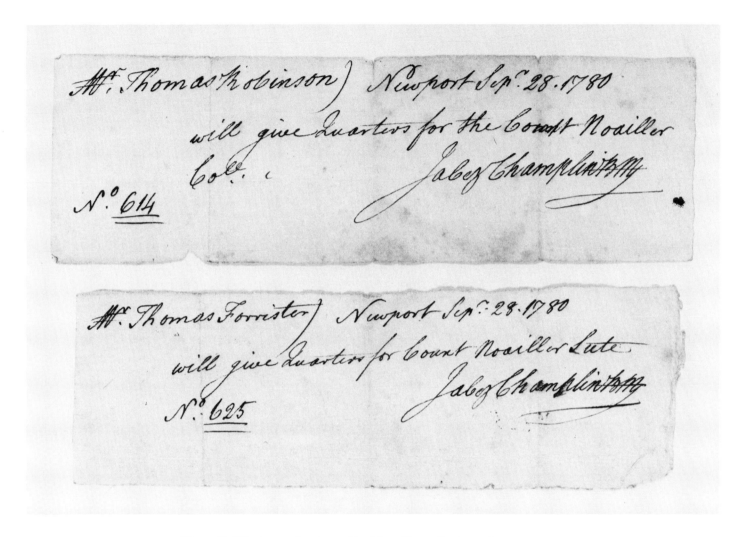

Figure 12. Billeting notices issued by Jabez Champlin, barrackmaster, to householders in Newport. Thomas Robinson in house no. 614 was to quarter the Vicomte de Noailles; Thomas Forrister in house no. 625 the vicomte's servants ("sute"). Courtesy, Henry Austin Wood, descendant of Thomas Robinson and owner of his house on Washington Street.

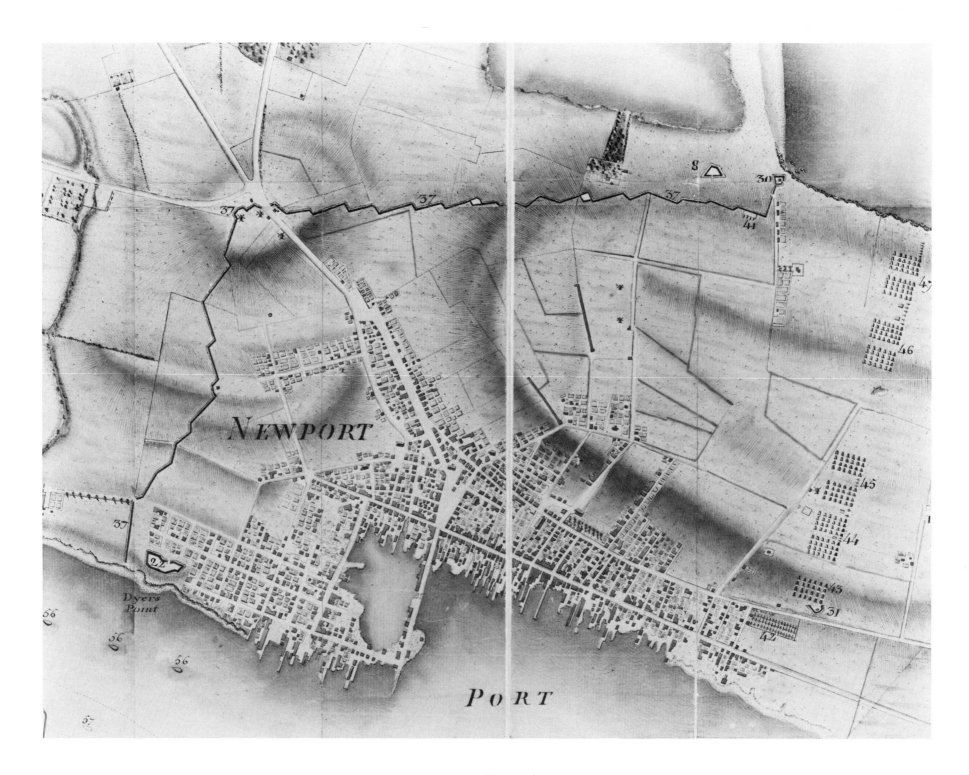

NEWPORT

Dyers
Point

PORT

None of the excellent maps of Newport drawn by the French engineers in the fall of 1780 was labeled a map "to prepare for the establishment of winter quarters." They were all primarily concerned with fortifications. But Desandroüins's map (*Figure 13*) with its meticulous town plan could have served as a guide to billets, and an even better map for this purpose, from which Desandroüins must have borrowed, was a town plan by Charles Blaskowitz that had been engraved in London in 1777 and was brought to Newport by Rochambeau's engineers.[34] (*Figure 14*)

Organizing winter quarters in Williamsburg must have been both easier and harder than it had been in Newport. Easier because the French had done it all before, and because a victorious ally had a stronger claim on American gratitude than an untried one; harder because they had so little time in which to get organized and so much difficulty in reaching the town council before civilians had returned to the town and while soldiers were still on service. Williamsburg was also much smaller, a prewar population of fifteen hundred when the assembly was not in session compared with nine thousand in Newport and about two hundred and fifty dwellings compared with the seven hundred that remained in Newport after the British occupation had destroyed as many as four hundred.

Notwithstanding these differences in scale and situation, the billeting practices must have had a good deal in common. In Virginia, as in Rhode Island, most of the men were barracked in repaired houses while the officers were lodged in private homes. The roles of the barrackmasters must have been very similar. Formal billeting lists may not have been needed for Yorktown, Jamestown, or West Point,[35] where the number of officers involved was so small, but the headquarters staff that was quartered in Williamsburg was the same staff, with a few additions and subtractions, for whom billeting lists had been compiled in Newport and Providence. A billeting list for Williamsburg, and a file of the notices sent by the barrackmaster to Williamsburg householders, should be postulated even though no trace of them has survived apart from the apparent allusion to a list (*Etat*) in the graffiti. It should be remembered that if it were not for the chance survival of two billeting notices in Newport, out of the hundreds that Champlin must have signed, the historian would still know nothing of this procedure.

The answer to Puzzle 4—How Was It Used?—has now been suggested as far as the map's purpose is concerned. We may assume that the Frenchman's Map—and its lost successor—was on file in whatever house de Béville and his staff used as their office, together with whatever billeting lists had been accumulated for all the officers and men quartered in the town. The town plan being as simple as it was, and the streets on the map so plainly marked, it must have been easy with a little practice to locate a billet. If anything more were needed, it could only have been a simple street key, attached to the map, which listed the officers and men housed on each street.

It is an intriguing question whether the houses occupied by Frenchmen in Williamsburg were assigned a number, as we know they were in Newport and as they seem to have been in Hampton. Could the Wythe House in Williamsburg have had its number, just as the Vernon House in Newport, where Rochambeau spent his first winter, had been num-

Figure 13. Town plan of Newport, R.I., drawn by Desandroüins in the summer of 1780 as part of a very large map of French positions. It could have served as a billeting map. Courtesy, Collections of Geography and Map Division, Library of Congress.

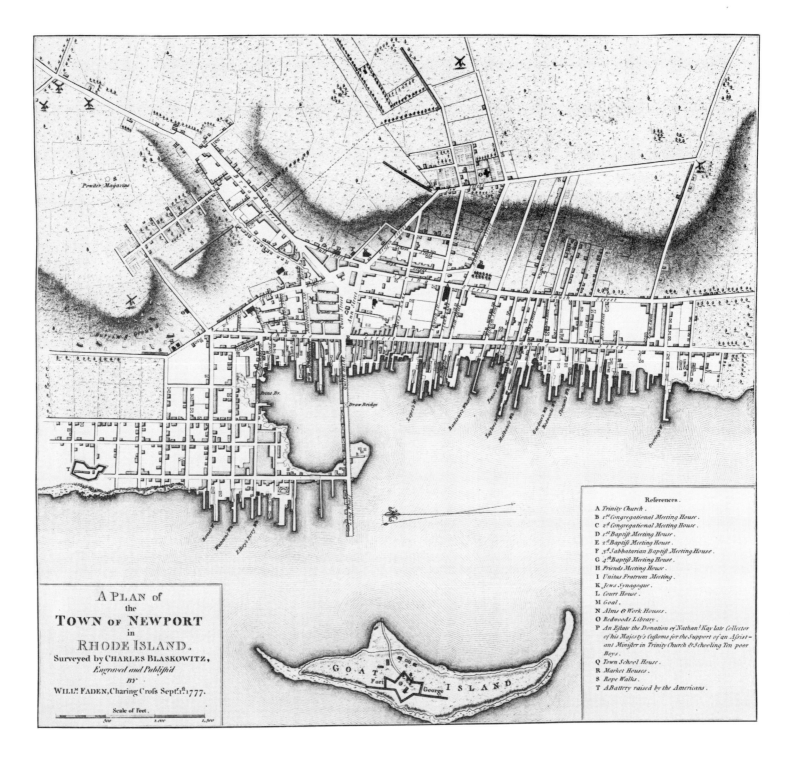

References.

A Trinity Church.
B 1st Congregational Meeting House.
C 2d Congregational Meeting House.
D 1st Baptist Meeting House.
E 2d Baptist Meeting House.
F 3d Sabbatarian Baptist Meeting House.
G 4th Baptist Meeting House.
H Friends Meeting House.
I Unitas Fratrum Meeting.
K Jews Synagogue.
L Court House.
M Goal.
N Alms & Work Houses.
O Redwoods Library.
P An Estate the Donation of Nathanl Kay late Collector of his Majesty's Customs for the Support of an Assistant Minister in Trinity Church & Schooling Ten poor Boys.
Q Town School House.
R Market Houses.
S Rope Walks.
T A Battery raised by the Americans.

A PLAN of
the
TOWN OF NEWPORT
in
RHODE ISLAND.
Surveyed by CHARLES BLASKOWITZ,
Engraved and Publish'd
BY
WILLM FADEN, Charing Cross Septr 1st 1777.

Scale of Feet.
500   1,000   1,500

GOAT ISLAND

Fort George

24

bered 302? If no billeting list for Newport had survived, it would still be known that the French had assigned numbers to houses in Newport, either from the publications of their naval printing press, with the house number 641 printed on them, or from several advertisements in the *Newport Mercury* of houses for sale which carried a "French" number. On the whole, it seems unlikely that scores of Williamsburg houses could have been given such numbers without a single instance coming down to us.

A Prototype Map?

Billeting was the primary use of the Frenchman's Map. But if we are right about the date of its composition, then it must have been available for consultation by every Frenchman who drew a map of Williamsburg after, let us say, November 1, 1781. It might, for example, have been an important source for Desandroüins's map. Desandroüins and de Béville were both quartered in Williamsburg after they left their field headquarters at the siege of Yorktown; their staffs must have seen each other almost daily and borrowed freely from each other's work. The same may have been true of the other official cartographers because they all had access to the same common stock of maps. In this way, an important secondary use for the Frenchman's Map, and for whatever further copy developed from it, may have been its contribution to several other "reenactment maps."

The only way to test this possibility is to compare these different town plans, of which there were perhaps five in all, not counting the Frenchman's Map. None of them is an original field map—that is to say, they were drawn after the event from notes, sketches, and any other available source including new surveys with the intent of commemorating a great triumph for French arms. They were the work of draftsmen with a keen professional pride and a strong sense of loyalty to their own commands.

We have encountered two of their authors before, Colonel Desandroüins and Alexandre Berthier, who was no doubt helped by his brother Charles. Another was Michel Capitaine du Chesnoy, a major in the Continental Army who was an aide-de-camp to Lafayette and drew several maps for him. The fourth was an aide-de-camp who performed the same office for the Marquis de Saint Simon. What they have in common is that all their maps, whether confined to the area around Williamsburg or extending over the peninsula, include a plan of the town. Major Capitaine's map and one of Berthier's two maps are campsite maps that do not take in much more area than the Frenchman's Map. Desandroüins's great map of the environs of Williamsburg includes more territory but not as much as the campaign maps by Saint Simon's cartographer and by Alexandre Berthier, both of which illustrate developments from the arrival of their armies in September to the battle of Yorktown.

We may begin with Capitaine's map *(Figure 15)* because Lafayette's army was the first to reach Williamsburg on September 6. An original manuscript is in the Engineers' Library at Paris.[36] Another copy, signed with his name, hangs on the wall of the Parish House at Bruton Church in Williamsburg. No one knows how it got there. His treatment of the town plan is very bland. It is mostly composed of those big, rectangular blocks painted in a flat red wash that the mapmaker used when he felt no need, or perhaps no

Figure 14. Town plan of Newport, R.I. Drawn for the British Admiralty by Charles Blaskowitz, this served as a base map for several others. Courtesy, Cornell University Library.

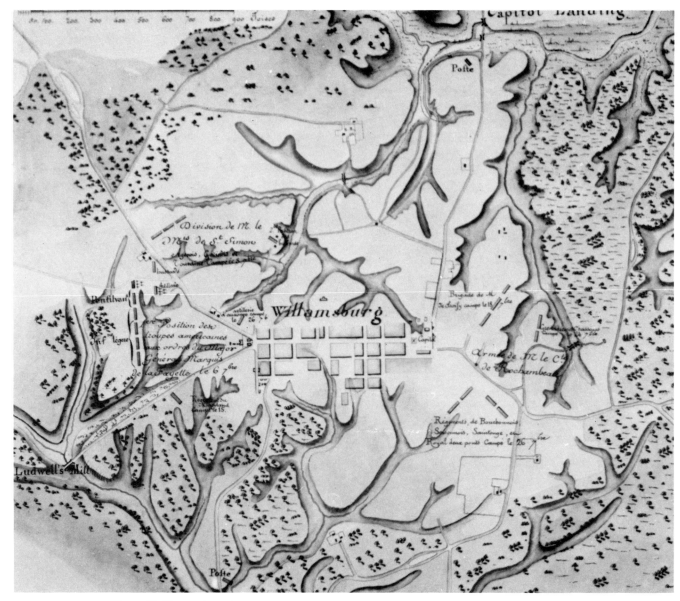

Figure 15. Town plan of Williamsburg drawn by Major Capitaine, aide-de-camp of Lafayette.

capacity, to go into detail. Although the Palace and the Capitol are indicated, the only building with a fairly specific symbol is the college where Lafayette was billeted and this map was probably begun. If it owes anything to the Frenchman's Map, the evidence does not show. It could, of course, have been finished before our map was started.

Some of the same uncertainty must be felt about the Saint Simon campaign map.[37] (Figure 16) This army joined Lafayette's on September 8 and was camped nearby. The cartographers may have worked together. Their treatment of creeks, streets, and military formations is virtually identical. But the town plan in Saint Simon's map goes into more detail. Church, Magazine, and Courthouse show up more clearly; house lots are fenced with dotted lines; several buildings are suggested; and there is one striking particular that is completely missing from Capitaine's town plan—the twin line of dots marking an avenue of catalpa trees leading up to the Palace that is such a conspicuous feature of the Frenchman's Map. Borrowing? Perhaps so, perhaps not. If so, it had to be done before November 4 when Saint Simon's forces left for the West Indies.

The presumption of borrowing may be carried much further in Berthier's two maps, both of which were done at leisure during the winter. The campsite map (Figure 7) was the last in an elegant series to illustrate the march from Providence to Williamsburg—the thirty-ninth site, where they camped on September 26. The campaign map is the unfinished peninsula map whose possibilities for the elucidation of the topography between Williamsburg and Yorktown stimulated this study. The plan of Williamsburg is in the finished portion. It is the tiniest of these five town plans, but it is done with great delicacy. To appreciate its detail it is necessary to study the original manuscript at the Château de Gros Bois because it cannot be seen in Rice's reproduction.

Berthier's technique was a compromise between the "bland block" treatment and the effort to distinguish an individual building, either inside or outside the fenced lots, with a little red block. The contrast between his detail and that of either Lafayette's cartographer or Saint Simon's can be appreciated by comparing what they make of the Palace. If we look first at Berthier's campsite map, we see a drawing with firm fence lines and clear symbols for the main building and its two dependencies as compared with the very simple token that the other two had used. This device of Berthier's might easily have been inspired by the diagram on the Frenchman's Map. But when we examine the manuscript of the campaign map with a magnifying glass, we are astonished to find that he seems to have gone back to the Frenchman's Map for even more detail. On the one hand, he has picked up the twin line of dots for the avenue of trees that were not on his campsite map. On the other hand, he has picked up an L-shaped building at the top of the Palace, believed to have been an orangery,[38] that was also missing from his other map. The same impression is confirmed by some other "new" particulars on the town plan of the campaign map. Miniscule as all this evidence is, it seems clear proof of "borrowings" unless there are other sources from which the same information might have been derived.

Finally, we come to Desandroüins's masterpiece, a campsite map (Figure 17) as its title indicates but one of extraordinary amplitude and precision. It was not

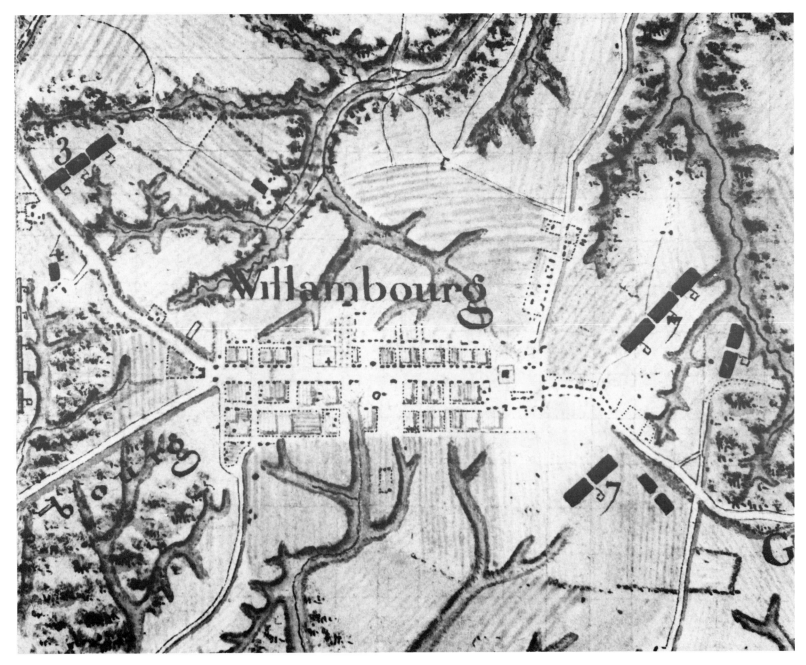

Figure 16. Town plan of Williamsburg by an aide-de-camp of Saint Simon. Courtesy, Newberry Library, Chicago.

completed until 1782 as can be seen not only from the date above the title but also from the reference to the accidental burning of the Palace, an event that occurred on December 22, 1781.

A comparison of this town plan with the Frenchman's Map reveals a point-by-point identity, or near-identity, in feature after feature, lot after lot, building after building. But there are also differences. Some are matters of scale. Desandroüins could not avoid the use of the "bland block" technique, although he shows many more buildings than anyone except the "unknown Frenchman." Some of the differences are matters of style and finish. Desandroüins chose to show tombs in the churchyard, rows of cannon near the Magazine, and gardens by several of the houses. He has used conventional signs for the trees leading up to the Palace, not little dots. He has a legend with a numbered key that removes the need to insert the name of a building on the map, but the same names will be found in the margin, with only two marked differences as compared with the names on the Frenchman's Map. Like Berthier and most Frenchmen at that time, Desandroüins referred to the Palace as "Gouvernement" (Government House); it was Americans and Englishmen who almost always called it the Palace. Desandroüins also omitted, as did everyone else except the "unknown Frenchman," any designation of the Wythe House as headquarters, perhaps because Washington hardly had had time to organize it as such before he set up his field headquarters at Yorktown.

More significant, perhaps, than any of these differences is the frequent variation that we find in the number and arrangement of all the little blocks that

Figure 17. Town plan of Williamsburg by Desandroüins. The numbers included in this portion are explained by his key as follows: 1. Government house 2. Courthouse 3. Capitol (divided by fold in map) 4. Church 5. College 6. Powder Magazine 7. Hospital 13. Rochambeau's troops 15. Rochambeau's artillery. Courtesy, Collections of Geography and Map Division, Library of Congress.

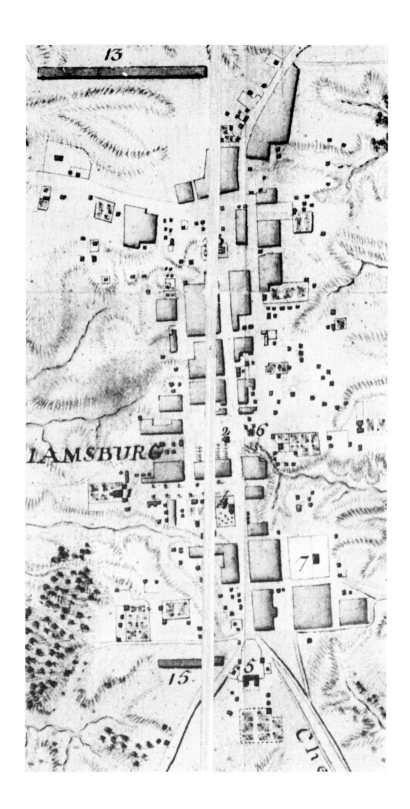

represent buildings. Only a specialist in the architectural history of the restoration of Colonial Williamsburg who knows the history of every house lot and the sources from which that history is derived could say how significant these differences are.

We can now sum up this comparative review. What are the alternative explanations of the striking similarities we find between the town plans of some of the reenactment maps and the Frenchman's Map?

We may think that the cartographers reached similar results by making their independent surveys without drawing in any way on each other's work. But this seems highly unlikely given the intimacy of this close-knit community and the comparatively few mapmakers involved. The first Frenchman to do a town plan of Williamsburg may have done it largely on his own, and, if he were in a hurry, his plan would be as general as Capitaine's was. But each would be available to a successor, and, once well under way, the Frenchman's Map must have displaced any other model as the most thorough and up-to-date map available.

It is also possible that these Frenchman had access to some town map or surveyor's plats that have since been lost.[39] Almost every county in Virginia and several cities had a surveyor whose business was drawing plats, and we know that Williamsburg had a town surveyor in 1774 named Matthew Davenport, one of whose manuscript plats has survived. But these plats, as can be seen from several eighteenth-century town plans, were almost always of lots and their owners.[40] They rarely showed a building. So, on the whole, there seems every reason to suppose that the Frenchman's Map did indeed serve as a prototype map for the work of Berthier, Desandroüins, and others.

It is also extremely interesting to consider whether a parallel case, reinforcing this conclusion by analogy, might not be drawn from a study of the siege maps of Yorktown with a view to determining how far they may have been influenced by a billeting map.

There was an old town plan of Yorktown but it was a plan of lots, not buildings. Many of the early siege maps had no plan to speak of, apart from an impression of Main Street, the cross streets, and a ravine or two. The sketch map that Querenet de la Combe, acting chief of the royal engineers, dashed off to France with his official report on October 20, the day after the surrender, showed no houses. The superb freehand map of the siege that the Berthier brothers hurriedly drew about the same time showed no houses. *(Figure 18)* Another great map entitled "Plan of Cornwallis's Army attacked and captured in Yorktown drawn on the spot by the engineers of the army" which was engraved in Paris by December was equally innocent of a town plan. Two of Washington's officers, Lieutenant Colonel Jean-Baptiste de Gouvion and Major Sebastian Bauman, had rushed in with their siege maps by October 29, with only rudimentary plans of the town. But then come two maps with an identical town plan that is clearly the work of a careful survey, one by Croublier d'Opterre to accompany an expanded version of the official engineers' report,[41] the other under the command of Colonel François-Marie d'Aboville of the French artillery. *(Figure 19)* Who made this survey? It is far from certain, but the answer could be Alexandre Berthier, whose survey for his billeting map of Yorktown preceded November 12, the date carried by his "display" copy. If so, then the billeting map for Yorktown was serving the same function we have ascribed to the billeting map for Williamsburg.

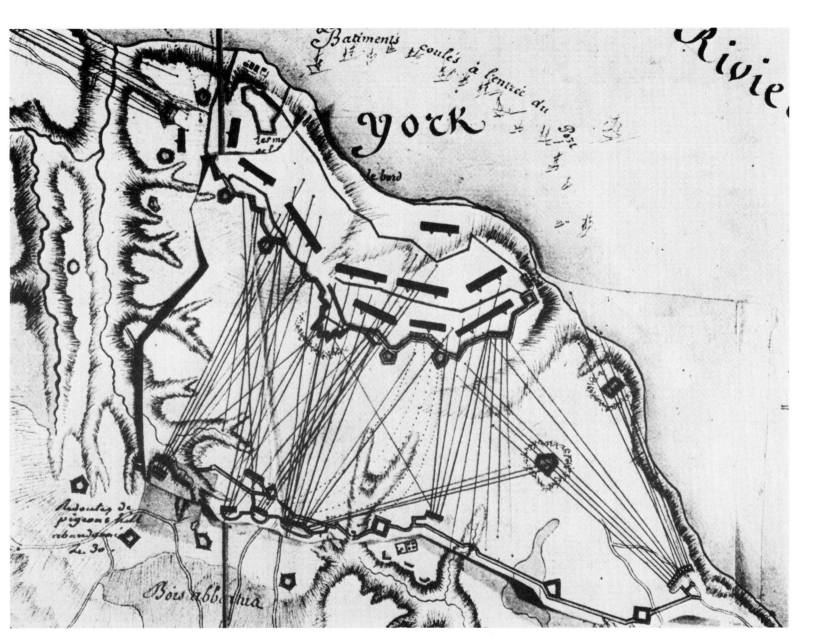

Figure 18. Detail from the freehand "Plan of the Siege of York" by the Berthier brothers in which almost no town plan is included. It is reproduced in Howard C. Rice, Jr., and Anne S. K. Brown, trans. and eds., *The American Campaigns of Rochambeau's Army, 1780, 1781, 1782, 1783,* II, Map 87. Courtesy, Princeton University Press.

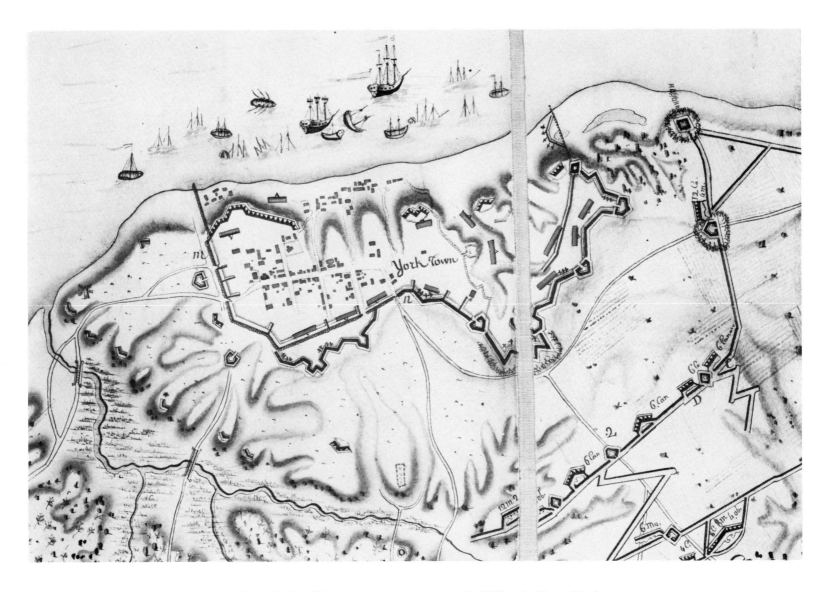

Figure 19. Detail from a manuscript map entitled "Plan du Siege d'York en Virginie par l'armee des G^aux Washington et Comte d'Rochambeau. Contre l'Armee Angloise Commandee par Lord Cornwallis en Octobre 1781." Streets and buildings are very similar to those on the Berthiers' billeting map *(Figure 6).* Courtesy, John Carter Brown Library.

Puzzle 5. Who Was the Author?

The game of authors was played with great enthusiasm in the early days of the Restoration, as we might expect, but for several decades now it has seemed as if the mantle of anonymity would never be lifted from "The Unknown Frenchman's Map."

It is a discouraging fact that of the scores of maps of the Yorktown campaign which can be examined today in the libraries of the United States, France, and Britain, less than 10 percent carry any designation of the author on the map itself and not more than another 10 percent can be safely attributed to an individual draftsman on the basis of other evidence.

Desandroüins's maps—whether done by him or for him—often carried his signature in the margin. The Berthier brothers signed their siege map below the border with the scribble "drawn freehand by the Berthier brothers in haste." Aides of Rochambeau, such as Mathieu Dumas or the Baron von Closen, signed some of their maps. So did French engineers under Desandroüins, like Querenet de la Combe and Croublier d'Opterre, or French engineers in the American service like Colonel Gouvion. Major Sebastian Bauman dedicated his siege map to Washington. The author's name was sometimes cited in the legend of a manuscript map or of an early engraved map; examples were Capitaine and Pechon, two aides of Saint Simon, and the English surveyors, Fage, Hills, and Hayman.

Other maps might be acknowledged in French letters or journals. Baron von Closen describes how he made a copy of a map of Portsmouth, Virginia, that Mathieu Dumas brought back with him after destroying the fortifications. Alexandre Berthier explains in his journal how he came to draw his map of Rhode Island. The billeting maps of Hampton and Yorktown were ascribed to Alexandre Berthier because they were found in his papers. Maps accompanying a journal have been assigned to its author, sometimes on dubious grounds.

Maps may be attributed on the basis of style. Obviously these Frenchmen could often have identified each other's work on this basis, and even today we may think that a particular treatment of woods and creeks or the formal border used to set off a display piece carries its own signature. Maps also come in families because so many of the good maps were copied either for multiple use or for security reasons, and a common authorship is recognizable even though copies are unsigned. A unique spelling can identify an author. More than one map done under Saint Simon's command is probably the work of his aide, Pechon, because he spells Cheesecake Church (originally Kiskiak Church) "Tyskae Kurtz."[42]

But maps thus identified are only a small proportion of all that survive and the only other test that might be used, handwriting where it is available, has its problems. The writing on the Frenchman's Map, which is informal handwriting, may be the work of a clerk. Copybook writing baffles identification because it eliminates all the idiosyncracies. Students of M. Paillasson or M. Roland were not trained to be themselves. They were trained to be beautiful, and beauty according to their masters had only three faces—the styles taught in this classical school by the names "ronde," "bâtarde," and "coulée."[43] So sufficient samples of informal handwriting on a map, deemed to be the author's own hand, which can be compared with similar samples of the writing of known cartographers, are a prerequisite for this test.

It is not surprising that the early enthusiasm cooled and that the game of authors, after the players had lost several rounds, was given up in the 1940s. However, with so much more scholarship available today it seemed worth playing again, but this time with two authors, not just one, to be found.

On the American side of the team, an interesting name showed up. Harold Gill of the Research Department at Colonial Williamsburg found that a surveyor, Robert Andrews, had been hired immediately after the Declaration of Independence in 1776 to draw plans for the construction of several barracks in Virginia. The *Journals of the Council* showed that on July 20 he and his assistant were paid £149 12s. 6d. "for making a survey and draught of the Posts of Williamsburg, York, Hampton, etc." If Andrews were still in business in 1781, he would have been a logical candidate for the choice of a surveyor to help in the construction of the Frenchman's Map. Gill also discovered that in 1778–1779 John Carter, of Carter's store in Williamsburg, was serving as a barrackmaster for the Williamsburg garrison.[44] If he were available in 1781, Carter could have been a candidate for the position of barrackmaster on Rochambeau's staff.

These were stimulating discoveries, but they were inconclusive compared with the startling progress on the French side, which was made in three exhilarating leaps.

The first jump was to realize that the pool of eligible candidates was really very small. It wasn't as if there were a good draftsman in every French platoon. There were probably not more than a score of French officers at the siege of Yorktown who could have drawn the Frenchman's Map, and several of them had disappeared with the armies of Saint Simon, Lafayette, and Washington before there was time to finish it. If it had been commissioned as a billeting map and had not been just the diversion of some officer, it must have been ordered by Rochambeau himself, or by de Béville, or by Querenet de la Combe (if Desandroüins, sick during the battle, were still out of action), or by some other senior staff officer. This reduces the available talent to a half-dozen royal engineers, two or three aides of Rochambeau's "family" who could draw a good map, two or three assistant quartermasters, and a couple of artillery officers. Moreover, thanks to a list of the staff officers at headquarters like the Newport billeting list, we already knew most of these officers by name and with luck could identify the others.

The second jump was to realize that it wasn't as if any of the above might have been given the assignment in the normal course of events. When this decision was made in the camp outside Yorktown with every staff officer running around like crazy if he were not recovering from a victory dinner of the night before, whose business was billeting? This investigation has shown repeatedly, at Newport, Providence, on the marches, and in Virginia, that it was the business of the quartermaster general and his staff. The royal engineers and the royal corps of artillery were far too busy with their own mopping-up after the battle to be asked to do someone else's job.

This thought started a furious search that was eventually rewarded by the discovery of a single sentence in a French diary which tells almost all. It appears between entries for October 21 and 24 in a journal kept by William, Comte de Deux Ponts, who was one of the two senior officers chosen by Rochambeau to carry the news of the victory back to France. It reads:

> Orders were given to the assistant quartermasters of the army to establish lodgings for the French army, which was immediately to take winter quarters, and to occupy the towns of Williamsburg, Hampton, Yorktown and Gloucester.[45]

This order uses the very same language that the Berthier brothers adopted in the titles of their billeting maps for Hampton and Yorktown and makes it virtually certain that the author of the Frenchman's Map, on the French half of the team, was an assistant quartermaster.

But which? The Newport and Providence billeting lists showed that de Béville's three assistants were Rochambeau's son, the Vicomte de Rochambeau, Rochambeau's nephew, Victor Collot, and Charles de Béville, the quartermaster general's own son. But others may have been in and out of the de Béville "family," especially as we know from Alexandre Berthier's own history that an officer might be asked to perform the duties of an assistant quartermaster before there was a vacancy in the establishment that he could fill. Was there any list that would show precisely who was functioning as an assistant quartermaster immediately after the Yorktown victory?

Among the Rochambeau manuscripts at the Library of Congress are de Béville's recommendations for rewards and promotions due to members of his staff at the end of the American campaigns. Signed by de Béville himself and annotated by Rochambeau, this manuscript took us right back to Puzzle 1 because the clerk who wrote it used the same variant figure 2

in his dates that appears on the Frenchman's Map! But whatever that might mean, there was no doubt about the importance of this document, entitled "Etat des Services," for the solution of Puzzle 5. Its discovery made the third leap possible.

De Béville had supplied a dossier for five individuals who were functioning as quartermasters after the siege. The first three were assistant quartermasters "on the establishment," two of them still being Victor Collot and Charles de Béville. The Vicomte de Rochambeau was now out of the picture, as was Charles, Chevalier de Lameth, an aide of Rochambeau's at Newport who had been promoted to assistant quartermaster and then severely wounded on October 14 at the siege of Yorktown. If he had been on his feet in Williamsburg instead of lying in hospital at the college, he would have been a serious candidate for the authorship. His vacancy had just been filled by Mathieu Dumas, who had also distinguished himself as one of Rochambeau's aides from the earliest days of the expedition. De Béville described all three as good draftsmen and surveyors who spoke English.

The remaining two had always acted as one, so perhaps we had four candidates, not five. These were Alexandre and Charles Berthier, aged twenty-seven and twenty-one. Charles was to die from his duel before this dossier reached the minister of war. Alexandre was the young man with the marshall's baton in his knapsack, the future chief of staff in an eighteen-year partnership with Napoleon. He had been made an "acting" assistant quartermaster on Rochambeau's staff in January 1781 in recognition of his superb map of Rhode Island. Charles had been given a staff appointment just after the siege, when Dumas's promotion created a vacancy. But they had been an inseparable team since they had made their own way to join Rochambeau in Newport in October 1780—brilliant sons of a brilliant self-made father whose family talent was mapmaking. De Béville's recommendation said they had been employed in this capacity throughout the whole campaign.[46]

Can any of these candidates be regarded as more likely than the others?

Figure 20. Alexandre Berthier about 1810 in his marshal's uniform. From a colored lithograph by Del Pech of a portrait by Jean Jacques François Monanteuil. Courtesy, Anne S. K. Brown Military Collection, Brown University.

There is a natural temptation to think first of the Berthier brothers because of their authorship of the Hampton and Yorktown maps. Williamsburg was the most important assignment. Would it not have been given to the ablest draftsmen? But there is a question of time, given the tight calendar postulated by this study. There is also the fact that the three maps are not absolutely uniform in style. And the informal handwriting on the Frenchman's Map is not, in Elizabeth McCarthy's opinion, identical with a sample shown her from Berthier's manuscript journal. If more of his *cahiers* should ever turn up to fill the tantalizing gaps in his journal that include the siege and the winter quarters in Williamsburg, the answer would no doubt emerge. But neither Rice nor the author of this study was able to find them among the leftover records at the Château de Gros Bois in Paris, the old residence that once contained the bulk of his papers.

If it should turn out to have been Alexandre Berthier (*Figure 20*), then there is no doubt which of the two surveyors on the Franco-American team was the shorter! Berthier always looked like a boy. At forty-two he was described as "short, stocky, always laughing, always bustling about."[47]

Dumas would be considered next (*Figure 21*). As a future general, a student of war and history as well as cartography, and the author of a journal, a good deal is known about him. Rochambeau had given him his staff appointment at Brest because he was a good draftsman, and one of his earliest assignments after reaching Newport in July 1780 was to draw an excellent freehand (*levé à vue*) "Plan of Newport and Vicinity" (*Plan de Newport et de ses Environs*) which he signed at the bottom in his own hand *"Dumas aide de camp fecit, le 12 juillet 1780."*[48]

This map included a miniature street map, without names but recognizable, the field camps of the French regiments and their artillery, and all the fortifications. In the fall Dumas was deeply involved in the plans for winter quarters, with the billeting of Lauzun's legion in Providence or Connecticut as his special assignment. While still an aide, he was a boon companion of the Berthier brothers and of Charles de Lameth, the assistant quartermaster whom he replaced. But he tells us in his memoirs that he was sent to Portsmouth immediately after Cornwallis's surrender with a detachment of Virginia militia to destroy the English fortifications there—a mission taking over a week. He has nothing to say of any assignment in Williamsburg beyond the fact that he was seldom there except to make reports and to visit his sick friend, de Lameth.[49]

Victor Collot was another future general who returned to America in 1796 as a paroled prisoner of war after being captured by the British while he was governor of Guadeloupe and was then sent by the French minister on a ten-month mission to survey the Mississippi Valley. This was semi-secret stuff, with an eye to the revival of French imperialism in Louisiana, of which nothing came. But it did produce two pioneer volumes in American cartography. The general was not a writing man, but nothing could be more absorbing than his record of his mission or more beautiful than the atlas of thirty-six maps and views that accompanied it. He had supervised the printing of all this before he died in 1805, but it was only published in Paris in 1826.[50]

Unfortunately there is nothing in Collot's narrative or in the style of his engraved maps to connect this work with the Frenchman's Map. No maps ascribed to Collot have survived from the Revolutionary War, and nothing is known about his activities beyond his direction of various divisions on the march, a duty that usually fell to one of the assistant quartermasters. Charles de Béville also took charge of columns and performed, no doubt, as well as his father said he did. But no maps whatever have been traced to him.

This is the end of the road. Any one of the four or five may have been given the Williamsburg assignment. There is even the unlikely possibility that another aide of Rochambeau's who could draw may have been pressed into service.[51] The hope that the identity of the unknown author of the Frenchman's Map, expressed in the dedication of the facsimile reproduction, may some day be revealed is still there to inspire another investigator.

Puzzle 6. The Map's Fate

To summarize what our guesswork has made of five of the six puzzles:

Puzzle 1. The date on the map is May 11, 1782. The date of its composition was sometime between the surrender of Cornwallis on October 19 and the entry into winter quarters at Williamsburg on about November 15.

Puzzle 2. It is a billeting map, like the billeting maps of Yorktown and Hampton.

Puzzle 3. It was probably arranged through the cooperation of a barrackmaster general, a Williamsburg man, and executed by a French engineer with the help of a local surveyor.

Examination of the manuscript suggests that it was a second draft, which was discarded after it was used to produce a more finished copy of which no trace has survived.

Puzzle 4. Its primary use was as a billeting map. A new look at the way in which Rochambeau organized his first winter quarters, in Newport, Rhode Island, in 1780–1781, reveals methods, maps, lists, and keys that must have influenced his second winter in Williamsburg.

It probably also served as a prototype, or base map, for all later French maps that included a town plan of Williamsburg.

Puzzle 5. Its French author was an assistant quartermaster general on the staff of Brigadier General de Béville, the French quartermaster general. He was one of five assistants whom de Béville is known to have had when the map is believed to have been drawn.

There is no good answer to Puzzle 6, which concerns the fate of this draft.

Early in May 1782 word of the impending move began to spread among the troops. This draft, gathering a little dust in the quartermaster general's office, had already attracted those faint, irreverent scribbles that are barely visible in a facsimile reproduction impressed with the dignity of history. It was probably on May 11, with a move in the air, that a filing clerk gave it a title and a date.

Toward the end of May the news of the birth of a male heir to the French throne reached the Atlantic seaboard and led to various complimentary addresses. The mayor, recorder, aldermen, and common council of the city of Williamsburg congratulated his excellency the Comte de Rochambeau on this happy event and then added their own praise for the deportment of their French guests:

The present occasion enables us also gratefully to acknowledge to your Excellency our obligation for that Discipline and Good Order which has been so strictly observed by the troops quartered in this City, and for that ready attention which has ever been shown to prevent an interference with the privileges and immunities of free citizens.[52]

How far this was in gratitude for past conduct and how far in anticipation of compensation for wear and tear does not appear. But we can be very certain that when the move finally came on July 1, 1782, it was the occasion for all sorts of parties and gaieties and many tender sorrows.

Perhaps the Frenchman's Map that we have was given to a local citizen—like St. George Tucker who had fought at the siege, or like the barrackmaster general—as a memento of all the experiences that Frenchmen and Americans had shared.

Perhaps it just lay quietly in some private library, like the one in the Robert Carter House near the Palace, which contained all sorts of letters and memorabilia of the Virginia heroes of the Revolution until the Union soldiers came to Williamsburg.

Perhaps this sort of history lies behind Dr. Swem's laconic remark, "Mr. Crimmins, according to Miss Christian, acquired it from someone who had taken it during the War Between the States." If the identity of the small library that Mr. Crimmins bought in Norfolk, with the map tucked in a book, had been recorded, it might have supplied a clue.

All that we really know about the fate of the Frenchman's Map after the French left Williamsburg is that it eventually surfaced within a few miles of where it had been drawn to tease the imagination of anyone who enjoys a good historical puzzle.

Notes

1. For Desandroüins's map of Williamsburg, see John R. Sellers and Patricia Molen Van Ee, comps., *Maps and Charts of North America and the West Indies, 1750–1789: A Guide to the Collections in the Library of Congress* (Washington, D.C., 1981), no. 1452. An excellent reproduction of the manuscript, by Historic Urban Plans (Ithaca, N.Y., 1975), is in the Library of Congress. For maps of Rhode Island by Desandroüins and the Berthiers, see Howard C. Rice, Jr., and Anne S. K. Brown, trans. and eds., *The American Campaigns of Rochambeau's Army, 1780, 1781, 1782, 1783,* 2 vols. (Princeton, N.J., 1972), II, pp. 126–127 and maps 6–9. For siege maps of Yorktown, see Sellers and Van Ee, comps., *Maps and Charts,* no. 1467 (Querenet de La Combe), no. 1472 (Captain Fage), or no. 1475 *(Carte des environs d'York).*

2. Rice and Brown, trans. and eds., *American Campaigns,* II, p. 160 and map 91. A forthcoming essay by the author, "Glimpses of a Lost World," is based on new photography of the original manuscript at the Château de Gros Bois, Paris.

3. Manuscripts and Rare Books, Earl Gregg Swem Library, College of William and Mary, Williamsburg, Va.

4. E. G. Swem to Harold Shurtleff, Dec. 12, 1935, Archives and Records, Colonial Williamsburg Foundation.

5. David Challinor to Alan Simpson, Apr. 3, 1983.

6. Goodwin to Rockefeller, Archives and Records, CWF.

7. E. G. Swem to Judge Hutcheson, Nov. 4, 1963, College Archives, Swem Library.

8. Oral history of Bishop John B. Bentley, College Archives.

9. *Ibid.*

10. For photographs, see album, Architecture Library, CWF. Copies of the correspondence are in Archives and Records, CWF.

11. E. G. Swem to Rutherfoord Goodwin, Nov. 9, 1937, Archives and Records, CWF.

12. This "window" is visible in photographs of 1972 taken before the fabric was removed. The W. J. Barrow Restoration Shop, Richmond, Va., has no record of Mr. Barrow's repairs.

13. Legend, first facsimile edition, printed by Meriden Gravure Co., copyrighted by CWF, and issued in 1945. The history of the loan of the map by the college to the Foundation in 1941 and of the preparation of the first facsimile edition was reviewed by CWF president Kenneth Chorley in a letter of Nov. 16, 1942, to John E. Pomfret, president of William and Mary. Archives and Records, CWF.

14. Donnelley's proposal for the conservation of the map was made by Harold W. Tribolet to Henry Grunder in a letter of July 5, 1972, Manuscripts and Rare Books, Swem Library.

15. Indispensable aids are Rice and Brown, trans. and eds., *American Campaigns,* Sellers and Van Ee, comps., *Maps and Charts,* John W. Reps, *Tidewater Towns: City Planning in Colonial Virginia and Maryland* (Williamsburg, Va., 1972), and John Bryan Harley, Barbara Bartz Petchenik, and Lawrence W. Towner, *Mapping the American Revolutionary War* (Chicago, 1978), which includes a valuable bibliography on pp. 173–182. Still useful are the photocopies of maps in French collections compiled by Professor Louis C. Karpinski of the William L. Clements Library, University of Michigan, Ann Arbor, in the 1930s. The Colonial National Historical Park library at Yorktown and the Research Center at CWF have good collections of photocopies from American and French sources. The Library of Congress has the most comprehensive collection of Rochambeau's manuscript maps in America. French collections visited for this study included the Bibliothèque Nationale, the Service Historique at the Château of Vincennes, the Engineers' Library at Paris (Inspection Générale du Génie) and their archives at Vincennes (Archives du Génie), and the Château de Gros Bois. Two French journals, not examined by Rice and Brown, were inspected in France and will be studied further— one by Rochambeau's aide, the Comte de Lauberdière, a first-class source for the campaigns of 1780, 1781, 1782, and 1783, with maps attached, recently deposited at the Bibliothèque Nationale, the other by Lt. Col. Claude-Etienne Hugan of Lauzun's legion, "Journal Hyver 1781 a 1782 Hampton, Charlotte etc.," which is at the Bibliothèque Municipale d'Evreux. American collections with items of special interest for this study that were visited included the John Carter Brown and John Hay libraries at Brown University, university libraries at Princeton, Harvard, Yale, and the University of Michigan, the Newberry Library, Chicago, the library of Paul Mellon, Upperville, Va., the United States Army Engineer Museum, Fort Belvoir, Va., and the historical societies of Massachusetts, Pennsylvania, Virginia, Rhode Island, and Connecticut.

16. Denis Diderot, *Encyclopédie ou Dictionnaire Raisonné des Sciences, des Arts et des Métiers,* XIX (Paris, 1763), pp. 159–166.

17. A. F. Roland, *Le Grand Art d'Ecrire,* with plates engraved by Le Parmentier (Paris, 1758), plate XVII. I owe my introduction to this work, and to the history of the writing academies, to James M. Wells of the Newberry Library.

18. See p. 35.

19. Rice and Brown, trans. and eds., *American Campaigns,* II, pp. 167–171, "Winter Quarters in Virginia November 1781–June 1782."

20. Berthier Papers, no. 28 (Hampton), no. 29 (Yorktown); Rice and Brown, trans. and eds., *American Campaigns,* II, maps 99 and 106.

21. Journals of de Lauberdière and Lt. Col. Hugan.

22. The *toise* was 1,949 meters, equivalent to about 2 English yards or a fathom. The metric system was adopted in France in 1795. Rice and Brown, trans. and eds., *American Campaigns,* II, p. 120.

23. *Ibid.,* map 86.

24. Written on board the *Neptune,* Jan. 12, 1783, *ibid.,* I, p. 264.

25. MS map, Redwood Library, Newport, R.I.

26. Sellers and Van Ee, comps., *Maps and Charts,* no. 1470.

27. For further details, see pp. 20–25 and n. 33.

28. Correspondence du Comte de Rochambeau, A1-3734, p. 157, Service Historique, reprinted in Henri Doniol, *Histoire de la Participation de la France à l'Etablissement des États-Unis d'Amérique,* V (Paris, 1892), pp. 584-585.

29. The joins with their overlaps coincide with the horizontal and vertical folds in the manuscript. The center point is between the Courthouse of 1770 and the Powder Magazine.

30. The absence from the Frenchman's Map of any street names related to the monarchy such as Duke of Gloucester, Henry, Nicholson, and Francis, and the substitution of Main, Mill, North, and South for those names, might suggest an anti-British reaction of the sort that occurred in Newport, R.I., but if so, it was short-lived. In Newport, the first town council to meet in 1780 after the evacuation of the British in November 1779 substituted Congress Street for Queen's Street and Lewis Street (in honor of the French king) for King Street.

31. For guidance in this examination of the manuscript I am indebted to Paul Buchanan.

32. The French billeting lists for officers lodged in Newport and Providence in 1780–1781 were first published in an English translation by John Austin Stevens, "The French in Rhode Island," *Magazine of American History,* III (July 1879), pp. 423–431, from an original manuscript now in the Fraunces Tavern Museum, New York, N.Y. They were reproduced in French by Edwin Martin Stone, *Our French Allies* (Providence, 1884), pp. 220–224, 321–323.

33. Alan Simpson, "A New Look at How Rochambeau Quartered His Army in Newport (1780–1781)," *Newport History: Bulletin of the Newport Historical Society,* LVI (Spring, 1983). This article includes an updated translation of the Newport billeting list from the original manuscript sources.

34. Two copies of the version of Blaskowitz's map used by the French engineers, I. K. 360 and 369, are in the Mellon Library.

35. There were only three companies of artillery and a miners company at West Point, all under the command of Lt. de Chazelles. Lt. Clermont-Crèvecoeur, who was there, wrote, "West Point, otherwise known as Delaware, is a little hamlet of 7 or 8 houses at the confluence of the Mattaponi and Pamunkey rivers. We had great trouble finding lodgings. The soldiers occupied the abandoned houses, and eventually the officers were fairly comfortable. We built batteries on the two rivers and set up a bomb battery in between." Rice and Brown, trans. and eds., *American Campaigns,* I, p. 66. Maps 104 and 105 show houses that were no doubt used for billets. *Ibid.,* II.

36. "Position a Williamsburg de l'Armée combiné etc.," Atlas de la Guerre d'Amérique, NS A 224, Bibliothèque du Génie. The Bruton Church copy was reproduced as fig. 123 in Reps, *Tidewater Towns.*

37. *Carte de la Campagne de la Division aux ordres du Mis de St. Simon en Virginie.* Ayer Collection, Newberry Library.

38. Besides the Frenchman's Map, the only map known to have included this feature was not accessible to the French. It was reproduced by Reps from the papers of the English officer, Col. John Graves Simcoe. *Tidewater Towns,* fig. 101.

39. Paul Buchanan informs me that city tax maps were lost during the Revolution and not redrawn until 1800. It has also been suggested that certain omissions and discrepancies in the Frenchman's Map would not have occurred if the draftsman had had access to an accurate town survey. *Ibid.,* p. 152.

40. See plats of eighteenth-century towns reproduced *ibid.* Fig. 58 (Yorktown, 1691) is a plat of lots, as are figs. 103–106 (Williamsburg, 1800 and later). A public building occasionally appears on these maps as a roughly drawn structure.

41. "Journal du Siege d'York in Virginie, Carte No. 2," d'Opterre Manuscripts, Mellon Library.

42. Carte de la Campagne faite en Virginie en 1781 . . . Levé en Sep*bre* et Oct*bre* par Pechon, aide de camps de M*r* le M*is* de St. Simon. Ministère de la Guerre, L.I.D. 174 (Karpinski photocopies). This map is similar to the map in the Ayer Collection, but it does not have the view of York.

43. See James M. Wells, "The Bureau Académique d'Ecriture: A

Footnote to the History of French Calligraphy," *Papers of the Bibliographical Society of America*, LI (1957).

44. Treasurer's Office Receipt Book (1778–1779), TR 29, pp. 735, 819, Virginia State Library, Richmond.

45. *My Campaigns in America: A Journal kept by Count William de Deux-Ponts, 1780–81*, trans. Samuel Abbott Green (Boston, 1868), p. 152. The count sailed on Oct. 25, was pursued by the British, and started again on Nov. 1.

46. "Etat des Services de messieurs les officiers de l'Etat Major de l'armée employés dans l'Amérique Septentrionale," Rochambeau MSS, VI, pp. 645–650, Library of Congress. Collot, de Béville, and Dumas are classified as "Aydes Maréchaux Généraux des logis," i.e., assistant quartermasters general. The Berthiers are listed as "Adjoints a l'Etat Major de l'Armée," i.e., adjuncts to the army staff, but Rochambeau substituted "a la suite de l'état major" for "adjoint," which may have involved a difference in pay. Alexandre Berthier's initial appointment in Jan. 1781 had been as "aide maréchal général des logis surnuméraire," i.e., supernumerary. As their senior on the return voyage to France, Dumas, an assistant quartermaster general, refers to the Berthier brothers as "adjuncts to the general staff."

47. Rice and Brown, trans. and eds., *American Campaigns*, I, p. 201.

48. *Ibid.*, II, map 4.

49. Lieut.-Gen. Count Mathieu Dumas, *Memoirs of His Own Time* (Philadelphia, 1839), I, pp. 54–55.

50. Victor Collot, *A Journey in North America, Containing A Survey Of The Countries Watered By The Mississippi, Ohio, Missouri, etc. . . . illustrated by 36 Maps, Plans, Views and Divers Cuts . . .* (Paris, 1826). Authorities are not certain that the town plans in Collot's atlas were his own work. They have been ascribed to George Bois St. Lys, whose manuscript plans are in the Chicago Historical Society, American Philosophical Society, and Library of Congress.

51. Baron von Closen had been made an aide on his arrival in Newport because he was a good draftsman. Two other aides included in the "Etat des Services" were described as skillful draftsmen, de Lauberdière and Cromot Dubourg, who became an assistant quartermaster general early in 1782. There is no reference in their journals to any mapping assignment in Williamsburg.

52. Manuscript copies of Rochambeau correspondence, Vol. 3754, fol. 189, Service Historique.